P9-DJV-363

REGENCY PROFESSIONAL EDITION

prNpls v spdri srhN*

Joe M. Pullis, Ed.D.

Professor, Department of Office Administration and Business Communication
College of Administration and Business
Louisiana Tech University

New York, New York Columbus, Ohio Woodland Hills, California Peoria, Illinois

*PRINCIPLES OF *Speedwriting*® SHORTHAND

System Consultant:
Cheryl D. Pullis, M. Ed.

Contributors:
Linda Bippen
Peggy Runnels

Glencoe/McGraw-Hill
A Division of The McGraw-Hill Companies

Printed in the United States of America.

Send all inquiries to:
Glencoe/McGraw-Hill
21600 Oxnard Street
Woodland Hills, CA 91367-4906

ISBN 0-02-685100-8 (Student Text)
ISBN 0-02-685110-5 (Student Transcript)
ISBN 0-02-685120-2 (Instructor's Guide)

16 17 18 19 20 21 004 06 05 04

CONTENTS

What *Speedwriting* *Shorthand* Is

You are about to study *Speedwriting Shorthand*, a shorthand system that is based primarily on what you already know—the alphabet—to represent the sounds that make up our language.

Since you already know the alphabet, you will not spend much time retraining your mind and your hand to write the shorthand outlines. Instead, you will concentrate on applying the principles, or rules, of *Speedwriting Shorthand* to words commonly used in business. Taking notes, building speed, and transcribing dictation will be accelerated as a result. In a short period of time, you will be writing shorthand as easily and naturally as you now write longhand.

As you study *Speedwriting Shorthand*, you will also learn techniques for practicing and writing your shorthand quickly and successfully. Begin today to develop good writing and study habits. The dedication that you give to learning and practicing your shorthand will help assure success in your career.

BEFORE YOU BEGIN

Efficiency in taking dictation begins with selecting the appropriate writing tools.

Choose your pen carefully. Use a good ball-point pen. A pen glides more easily across paper than a pencil does, so you will save time and energy with each stroke. Always have more than one pen ready—in case the first one stops writing during dictation.

Use a steno-pad. A shorthand steno-pad is spiral bound at the top so that pages will flip easily and the book will lie flat while you are writing.

A line down the center divides the page in half. Write on only one side of the page until that side is filled. Then move to the other side of the same page. When you have filled the entire page, flip the paper and continue writing on the next blank page. When you have reached the last page of the notebook, turn it over and begin writing from back to front using the same procedure.

LESSON 1

Streamline letters as you write. Every time you lift your pen to cross a *t* or dot an *i*, you lose valuable time and reduce your speed. *Speedwriting Shorthand* eliminates extra strokes by avoiding loops, dots, and crosses whenever possible. As you practice, you will become comfortable with this technique, and you will find that streamlining letters makes writing faster, easier, and just as easy to read. Look at these examples:

t	b
f	i
j	y
g	p
h	z

1. Write what you hear.

The English language contains many silent letters. In longhand you write h-i-g-h even when you hear only the sound *hi* and k-n-o-w when you hear only *no*. In shorthand you write what you hear: hi and no. In the following examples, each word is followed by the sounds that are written in shorthand. This feature is known as *sound-spelling* and will help you to learn and remember shorthand vocabulary.

fee, f-e fe	tie, t-i ti
free, f-r-e fre	tray, t-r-a tra
view, v-u vu	ate, a-t at
knew, n-u nu	sigh, s-i si

Using this principle, write the outlines for the following words:

see, s-e *se* pay, p-a *pa*

low, l-o *lo* fly, f-l-i *fli*

2. Drop medial vowels.

Medial sounds are sounds that fall in the middle of a word. In shorthand, do not write vowels that fall in the middle of a word.

build, b-l-d *bld* save, s-v *sv*

*legal, l-gay-l *lgl* *glass, gay-l-s *gls*

did, d-d *dd* bulletin, b-l-t-n *bltn*

budget, b-j-t *bjt* *grade, gay-r-d *grd*

*The shorthand letter for g is pronounced *gay*, so the sound-spelling would be gay-l-s for glass; gay-r-d for grade; l-gay-l for legal.

Using this principle, write the outlines for the following words:

given, gay-v-n *gvn* said, s-d *sd*

visit, v-z-t *vzt* paper, p-p-r *ppr*

3. Write initial and final vowels, those you hear at the beginning and the end of a word.

office, o-f-s *ofs* easy, e-z-e *eze*

ahead, a-h-d *ahd* ready, r-d-e *rde*

*do, d-u *du* often, o-f-n *ofn*

follow, f-l-o *flo* *few, f-u *fu*

*Note that *u* is used for the long vowel sounds of $\overline{oo}$ and $\bar{u}$.

Using this principle, write the outlines for the following words:

value, v-l-u vlu | enough, e-n-f enf

open, o-p-n opn | happy, h-p-e hpe

The three principles you have just learned will allow you to write many words you will encounter on your job. In the remaining lessons, you will learn more principles that will enable you to write other sounds quickly and easily. Before going on, practice these additional words. First, read the word aloud and spell it according to its sound: grow, gay-r-o. Then sound-spell the outline as you write it: grow, gay-r-o gro .

deposit, d-p-z-t dpzt | type, t-p tp

news, n-z nz | *review, re-v-u rvu

sell, s-l sl | knowledge, n-l-j nlj

written, r-t-n rtn | apply, a-p-l-i apli

lease, l-s ls | *reason, re-z-n rzn

benefit, b-n-f-t bnft | unit, u-n-t unt

*Since medial vowels are omitted, the word beginning *re* is represented by an r.

PUNCTUATION SYMBOLS

Use quick, distinct symbols to show punctuation in shorthand notes. To show capitalization, draw a small curved line under the last letter of the outline: Bill, bl .

Sue, s-u su | Ed, e-d ed

Dallas, d-l-s dls | Debbie, d-b-e dbe

Ted, t-d td | New Haven, n-u h-v-n nu hvn

To indicate a period at the end of a sentence, write \ .

Let Bill know. lt bl no \

To indicate a question mark, write ×.

Does Bill know? dz bl no ×

To indicate the end of a paragraph, write >.

Bill does know. bl dz no >

BRIEF FORMS

You will use some words so often that you will find it helpful to write shortened outlines for them. These shortened outlines are called **brief forms.** Since brief forms are not written in full, you should memorize them. Study and practice the brief forms until you can write them as quickly, easily, and accurately as you write your own name—without hesitation.

More than one word can be represented by the same brief form. When read in context, however, only one meaning will make sense.

a, an .	we e
will, well l	the
it, at	is, his
to, too l	in, not n

PRINCIPLES SUMMARY

1. Write what you hear: know, n-o no.
2. Drop medial vowels: build, b-l-d bld.
3. Write initial and final vowels: office, o-f-s ofs; ready, r-d-e rde.

WORD CONSTRUCTION

Practice writing these words. **Example:** desire, d-z-r dzr

above, a-b-v ________	travel, t-r-v-l ________
loan, l-n ________	delay, d-l-a ________
receive, re-s-v ________	let, l-t ________

supply, s-p-l-i ____________

help, h-l-p ____________

city, s-t-e ____________

held, h-l-d ____________

telephone, t-l-f-n ____________

offer, o-f-r ____________

READING AND WRITING EXERCISES

You now know enough shorthand to write complete sentences. Read the following outlines aloud. When you encounter an unfamiliar outline, sound-spell the word. If the correct word still does not come to mind, read on to the end of the sentence. The context, or meaning, of the sentence will help you identify the unfamiliar outline. If you are still unable to read the outline, look in the Student Transcript that accompanies your textbook.

Series A

1. e hp l se u sn.

2. l u pa . fe x

3. /) . nu fl unl.

4.) (unl l ll x

5. su l n flu l dls.

Series B

1. ed) n) ofs.

2. dd u rsv . bl x

3. ll dbe l pa / .

4. u l du l n . ofs jb.

5. e l gv u . rz n pa.

Series C

1.) bl / (ofs x

2. (rvu) eze l lp.

3. su l grd / \
4.) (nu bgl rde l rvu x
5. e dd n rsv / \

STUDY PLAN

As you work through each lesson, use these steps as a study plan:

1. Study the principles and the words illustrating each principle at the beginning of each lesson. Think about how the principle applies to each of the words listed under it.
2. Practice each word listed under the principle. First, say the word aloud: glass. Then sound-spell the word aloud as you would write it in shorthand: gay-l-s. Then sound-spell and write the shorthand outline for the word: gay-l-s gls . Write each word two or three times or until you feel comfortable writing the word.
3. Complete the exercises following the presentation of the principles.
4. Read the shorthand outlines in the Reading and Writing Exercises in the textbook until the material can be read easily. If the correct word for an outline does not immediately come to mind, read on to the end of the sentence. The context, or meaning, of the sentence will help you identify the unfamiliar outlines.

   Consult the Student Transcript if you cannot determine the correct word with the help of sound-spelling and context. Beginning with Lesson 3, each letter or memorandum in the Transcript is marked in groups of 20 standard shorthand words (28 syllables). Small, raised, consecutive numbers are placed after each group of 20 shorthand words. Thus, if while reading you are able to reach the number 4 in one minute, you would be reading at the rate of 80 words per minute (20 × 4). If you reach the number 5, you would be reading at the rate of 100 words per minute. As a general rule, you should be able to read about twice as fast as you expect to write from dictation.
5. Write the Reading and Writing Exercises from the Transcript while dictating to yourself.
   a. Read several words from the Transcript.
   b. Write the words while you sound-spell and say each word aloud.
   c. Repeat this procedure until you have written a letter or memorandum completely. Check the shorthand notes in the textbook for any outline that you may not know how to write.
   d. Read back the letter or memorandum from your own shorthand notes.

LESSON 2

1. Write c for the sound of *k*.

copy, k-p-e cpe
like, l-k lc
package, p-k-j pcj
school, s-k-l scl
clerk, k-l-r-k clrc
desk, d-s-k dsc

2. Write a capital C for the sound of *ch, cha* (pronounced *chay*).

change, chay-n-j Cnj
such, s-chay sC
chosen, chay-z-n Czn
teach, t-chay tC
check, chay-k Cc
church, chay-r-chay CrC

To write *m* and *w* with ease and speed, streamline the outlines.

3. Write ⌒ for the sound of *m*.

may, m-a ⌒a
name, n-m n⌒
mail, m-l ⌒l
much, m-chay ⌒C
my, m-i ⌒i
same, s-m s⌒

4. Write ◡ for the sound of *w* and *wh*.

way, w-a

when, w-n

what, w-t

winner, w-n-r

week, w-k

wage, w-j

where, w-r

which, w-chay

5. To add *ing* or *thing* as a word ending, underscore the last letter of the outline.

billing, b-l-ing

something, s-m-thing

watching, w-chay-ing

*paying, p-a-ing

attaching, a-t-chay-ing

*saying, s-a-ing

*Note: Always write long vowels before marks of punctuation.

6. To form the plural of any outline ending in a mark of punctuation, double the last mark of punctuation.

billings, b-l-ings

savings, s-v-ings

7. *Adding* s. Write s to form the plural of any outline ending in a letter: books, b-k-s bcs. Write s to form possessives: girl's, gay-r-l-s grls. Write s to add s to a verb: runs, r-n-s rns. Add s even though the final sound of such words may be z.

checks, chay-k-s

hopes, h-p-s

helps, h-l-p-s hlps

jobs, j-b-s jbs

Bill's, b-l-s bls

gives, gay-v-s gvs

An s is also used in the writing of proper nouns ending in s, even though the final sound may be z.

James, j-m-s jms

Ames, a-m-s ams

Burns, b-r-n-s brns

Charles, chay-r-l-s Crls

Practice writing these additional words:

care, k-r cr

claim, k-l-m clm

games, gay-m-s gms

course, k-r-s crs

room, r-m rm

units, u-n-t-s unts

truck, t-r-k trc

match, m-chay mC

buildings, b-l-d-ings bld

each, e-chay eC

training, t-r-n-ing trn

coverings, k-v-r-ings cvr

ABBREVIATIONS

Many abbreviations are so common that they come to mind automatically. *Speedwriting Shorthand* makes use of these abbreviations. Since you already know many of these abbreviations, you will be able to write them quickly from the beginning.

company co

president P

information inf

and +

vice president VP

return ret

catalog cat

BRIEF FORMS

are, our r

can C

for, full f

us s

of, have, very v

PRINCIPLES SUMMARY

1. Write c for the sound of *k*: copy, k-p-e cpe.
2. Write a capital C for the sound of *ch, cha*: check, chay-k Cc.
3. Write ⌒ for the sound of *m*: may, m-a ⌒a.
4. Write ◡ for the sound of *w* and *wh*: way, w-a ◡a; when, w-n ◡n.
5. To add *ing* or *thing* as a word ending, underscore the last letter of the outline: billing, b-l-ing bl̲; something, s-m-thing s⌒̲.
6. To form the plural of any outline ending in a mark of punctuation, double the last mark of punctuation: billings, b-l-ings bl̳.
7. Write s to form the plural of any outline ending in a letter, to form possessives, to add s to a verb: jobs, j-b-s jbs; Bill's, b-l-s bls; gives, gay-v-s gvs; or to write the final s of a proper noun: James, j-m-s j⌒s.

WORD DEVELOPMENT Write the shorthand outlines for the following related words.

Example: bill bl	-s bls	-ing bl̲	-ings bl̳
truck trc	-s ______	-ing ______	-er ______
keep cp	-s ______	-ing ______	-er ______
move ⌒v	-s ______	-ing ______	-r ______
follow flo	-s ______	-ing ______	-er ______
time t⌒	-s ______	-ing ______	-r ______
teach tC	-es ______	-ing ______	-er ______

WORD CONSTRUCTION Practice writing these words. **Example:** approaching, a-p-r-chay-ing aprC̲

cake, k-k ______	makes, m-k-s ______
because, b-k-z ______	planning, p-l-n-ing ______
case, k-s ______	while, w-l ______
nature, n-chay-r ______	water, w-t-r ______

could, k-d ________ future, f-chay-r ________

items, i-t-m-s ________ matter, m-t-r ________

READING AND WRITING EXERCISES

Series A

1. r u rde l du s— lp̲? / r inf arvs.

2. e l hlp u ufe c. / r , r jb.

3. r P + VP v r co / l se s n . — c.

4. du u v r nu / blln? r , v l / rln.

5. — C — c r u / pln̲ l vzl r ofs?

Series B

1. ll — e no — n / r inf arvs.

2. i l — l . f dpzl.

3. u l rsv . fre gfl / f eC sv̲ dpzl.

4. i l rel r Cc l / r co.

5. hr , . Cc l / cvr r fe n f.

Series C

1. e r — c̲ Cnjs / n r co cal.

2. e l — l u . cpe

v sn.

3. e s alC̲ . cpe
v r bl. —n c
u —l s . Cc?

4. bb̆ nds l no
s—̲ v sn.

5. i l lv r inf
/ , dsc.

LESSON 3

1. Write *m* for the sounds of *mem* and *mum*. Write *m* also for the sounds of *men, min, mon,* and *mun.*

memo, mem-o *mo*

members, mem-b-r-s *mbrs*

memory, mem-r-e *mre*

mumps, mum-p-s *mps*

menu, men-u *mu*

mineral, min-r-l *mrl*

monetary, mon-t-r-e *mtre*

money, mun-e *me*

2. Write *m* for the word endings *mand, mend, mind,* and *ment.*

demand, d-mand *dm*

amend, a-mend *am*

remind, re-mind *rm*

settlement, s-t-l-ment *stlm*

replacement, re-p-l-s-ment *rplsm*

judgment, j-j-ment *jjm*

*payment, p-a-ment *pam*

*agreement, a-gay-r-e-ment *agrem*

*Always write the final root-word vowel when adding word endings.

3. Write a capital *N* for the sound of *ent, nt* (pronounced *ent*).

sent, s-nt sN — entry, nt-r-e Nre

wants, w-nt-s Ns — renting, r-nt-ing rN̲

center, s-nt-r sNr — current, k-r-nt crN

Use N to form contractions.

don't, d-nt dN — couldn't, k-d-nt cdN

can't, k-nt cN — doesn't, d-z-nt dzN

Practice these additional words:

minimum, min-mum mm — front, f-r-nt frN

minutes, min-t-s mts — apparent, a-p-r-nt aprN

memorize, mem-r-z mrz — agent, a-j-nt ajN

mental, men-t-l mtl — didn't, d-d-nt ddN

recent, re-s-nt rsN — won't, w-nt N

PRINCIPLES SUMMARY

1. Write m for the sound of *mem* and *mum*: members, mem-b-r-s mbrs; mumps, mum-p-s mps. Write m for the sounds of *men, min, mon,* and *mun*: menu, men-u mu; minutes, min-t-s mts; monetary, mon-t-r-e mtre; money, mun-e me.
2. Write m for the word endings *mand, mend, mind,* and *ment*: demand, d-mand dm; amend, a-mend am; remind, re-mind rm; settlement, s-t-l-ment stlm.
3. Write a capital N for the sound of *ent, nt*: sent, s-nt sN; and for contractions: don't, d-nt dN.

WORD DEVELOPMENT

Write the shorthand outlines for the following related words.

pay pa — -ing ________ -ment ________ -ments ________

plant plN — -s ________ -er ________ -ing ________

agree *agre* -s ______ -ing ______ -ment ______

place *pls* -s ______ re- ______ -ment ______

rent *rN* -al ______ -ing ______ -er ______

settle *sll* -s ______ -ing ______ -ments ______

WORD CONSTRUCTION

Practice writing these words.

event, e-v-nt ______

different, d-f-r-nt ______

assignment, a-s-n-ment ______

central, s-nt-r-l ______

recommend, r-k-mend ______

pleasant, p-l-z-nt ______

member, mem-b-r ______

documents, d-k-ment-s ______

movement, m-v-ment ______

print, p-r-nt ______

memorizing, mem-r-z-ing ______

remember, re-mem-b-r ______

READING AND WRITING EXERCISES

1

mo l lvn crlr
l c gv u r inf u
nd l c r Cnjs
n r sls pln, l
v . cpe v r nu
pln C gvs f
dlls, / r crN
L r ofs, cp
. v bze scjl, e
r c plns f
s bg evNs f

c ‿cs ahd.
n cs u bri l
rC ‿e / ‿u
ofs i l lv c
cpes u nd / c
frN dsc, fl fre
l cl ‿e f hlp n
c fCr if u nd / .

2

mo l jde jcsn ‿u
mo, l rm u v r
plns l hld bgl hr
n c nr fCr, c
rzn f c hr, l rvu
nu bgl ilms + c
me e l nd l pa
f sC ilres. e r
‿c . scjl f eC
ofs. u l rsv .
nls asn u . dfnt
l‿, if u v nu
ilms or rplsms
pln l gv . brf
s‿re v eC / c
hr.

LESSON 4

1. Write for the sound of *ish* or *sh*.

finish, f-n-ish

machine, m-ish-n

should, ish-d

show, ish-o

wish, w-ish

issuing, i-ish-ū-ing

2. Write a capital for the word beginnings *ad* and *al* (pronounced *add* and *al* or *all*).

advise, ad-v-z

admit, ad-m-t

album, al-b-m

also, al-s-o

advice, ad-v-s

admire, ad-m-r

If a word begins with the letters *a-d* or *a-l* but does not incorporate the blended sounds of *ad* or *al* in the same syllable, write the word according to the sound.

adopt, a-d-p-t

align, a-l-n

3. Write for the initial sound of *en* or *in* (pronounced *n*).

anything, en-e-thing

engine, en-j-n

indent, in-d-nt *ndN*
involve, in-v-l-v *nvlv*
engineers, en-j-n-r-s *njnrs*
intent, in-t-nt *ntN*

BRIEF FORMS

from *f*
manage *—y*
firm *fr*
on, own *o*
part, port *pl*
letter *L*
would *d*
perhaps *Ph*
market *—r*
your *u*

BRIEF FORM DEVELOPMENT

Use brief forms and abbreviations to build related words. For instance:

Brief Form: *for*

form, for-m *f*
inform, in-for-m *nf*
formal, for-m-l *fl*
formula, for-m-l-a *fla*
fortune, for-chay-n *fCn*

Brief Forms: *can* and *not*

cancel, can-s-l *csl*
cannot, can-not *cn*

Abbreviation: *company*

accompanying, a-company-ing *aco*
accompaniment, a-company-ment *acom*

To avoid possible misinterpretations in reading and transcribing, write some outlines according to the rule rather than as derivatives of brief forms.

William, w-l-y-m *ly*
mechanical, m-k-n-k-l *—kncl*

NEW BRIEF FORM DEVELOPMENT

management *—ym*
manager *—yr*
managing *—y*
yours *us*
wouldn't *dN*
report *rpl*

marketing ⌒r̲ depart dpl
letters Ls letterhead Lhd

ABBREVIATIONS

Mr. ⌒r Ms. ⌒s
Mrs. ⌒rs Miss M

SALUTATIONS

Dear Mr. Gray d⌒r gra Dear Ms. Miller d⌒s ⌒lr
Dear Mrs. Chase d⌒rs Cs Dear Miss Temple d M ⌒pl
Dear Ed d ed Dear Sue d su

COMPLIMENTARY CLOSES

Sincerely yours su Very truly yours vlu
Cordially yours cu Yours truly ul
Sincerely s Yours very truly uvl
Cordially c Respectfully yours ru

PRINCIPLES SUMMARY

1. Write ꞩ for the sound of *ish, sh*: show, ish-o ꞩo .
2. Write a capital a for the word beginnings *ad* and *al*: advice, ad-v-s avs ; also, al-s-o aso .
3. Write n for the initial sound of *en* or *in*: entire, en-t-r ntr .

WORD DEVELOPMENT

Write the shorthand outlines for the following related words.

encourage ncrj -s ______ -ing ______ -ment ______
inform nf⌒ -s ______ -ing ______ -ant ______
furnish frnꞩ -es ______ -ing ______ -ings ______
short ꞩrl -s ______ -age ______ -ages ______

shop *sp* -s ______ -ping ______ -per ______

report *rpl* -s ______ -ing ______ -er ______

WORD CONSTRUCTION

Practice writing these words.

shown, ish-n ______

support, s-port ______

advising, ad-v-z-ing ______

increase, in-k-r-s ______

any, en-e ______

entire, en-t-r ______

efficient, e-f-ish-nt ______

brochure, b-r-ish-r ______

efforts, e-for-t-s ______

she, ish-e ______

afford, a-for-d ______

publishing, p-b-l-ish-ing ______

READING AND WRITING EXERCISES

1

mo l Crls gra r
rNl bld nd rpr.
e sd pN r ls
+ rpls r flr cvr
n eC r . e sd
aso rpls r s
sns n eC
unl, r ls ajN
dzN N s l rz
r rN. eC ls ,
crN. se , hp l
cp r bld f, l
, eds avs. i l
asc r ajN l gv
u . cl l sl . l
l so u eC bld.

2

d—rs Cs e v u L
aplı f . jb n r fr,
l u Aso —l s . L
—C gvs s infor /
lp + fl clss u v
lcn e —a v .
opn n r ofs sn,
f u inf e r alC .
cpe v r cos hr
plses, ll s no
—n u c vzl r fr,
e hp l hr f— u
sn, ul

3

d—r prcr i fgl l
—l —i pam l
u fr, i hp u l
fgv / dla, hr,
. Cc cvr pl v
/ bl, i l pa /
nlr bl v sn, s

4

mo l M su grn
i sN . nf—l L
l / P v / fr asc
l se . cpe v /
nu —r rpl, l
—i nlj e du n
yl v . rpli, d u
Aso rm / P e
dv —C lc l
no , plns f opn
r nu ofss / ,
L— l dsd o —C
frnt e l nd, e d
lc l v u Avs l,
ll —e no —n
u c —c / lrp
l r nu plN, i
Al lri l se u /
/ ofs —n u

arv.

5

ds hrpr Ph u
v n sn r nu
cal. if n l u
lc. fu mls l rd
r f e r alC ×
u l se e r so
me nu cls, if
u d lc l rsv.
cpe v r cal sn
r f + rel r l
r ofs. e l r+ r
cal l u, me ppl
lc l uz r cal l
sp r h. Nu
Cz r eze a l
sp l × cu

6

mo l bl dvdsn
e du n v. pln f
lrn r ppl l rn
r nu Ans. Ph
r plN yr + r
Cf nynr c hlp
dzn. pln e cd
uz f r ntr co.
ll s no l u
pln l du, Aso
l u l s. cpe
v u nu bgl × e
nd l rvu //
ym pln h.
Ph e c sv me n
r fCr if e lc
h l lc / eC
pl v r bgl.

LESSON 5

You will not have to change your basic handwriting style for *Speedwriting Shorthand*. However, it is important to develop writing habits that clearly distinguish one outline from another.

Take a moment now to review your writing style. Do you omit unnecessary loops, crosses, dots, and initial and final strokes where appropriate? Compare the following examples with the outlines you have written so far.

Streamlining *m* and *w*: Write *m* and *w* with a swift, smooth sweep of the pen.

m ⌒ me ⌒e

w ◡ way ◡a

Loops and Solid Lines: Write *l* with a clearly defined loop; write *t* with a solid stem. Your stroke for *t* should be clearly taller (about twice the height) than your *i*. The same is true for *l* and *e*, *nt* and *n*, *chay* and *k*.

l *l* t *t*

t *t* i *i*

l *l* e *e*

nt *M* n *n*

chay *C* k *c*

Closed Circles: It is important to close the circles in *s*, *d*, *p*, *gay*, and *a*.

s *s* sell *sl*

d *d* due *du*

p *p* pay *pa*

gay *g* get *gt*

a *a* aim *a*⌒

Stems on Tall Letters: Develop the habit of writing the stem long enough to distinguish *d* from *a*.

d	do
a	ache

Writing *s, ish, and* (ampersand): Develop a curve in the *s* to distinguish it clearly from the *ish*.

s	so
ish	show
ampersand	and

Streamlining Letters: Omit loops and upward strokes for *h, t, b, f, u,* and *i* when these letters occur at the beginning of an outline. Omit tails at the end of an outline.

h	hope
t	take
b	big
f	fine
u	unit
i	item

Writing *v* and *u*: The outline for the letter *v* ends with a brief tail at the top; *u* ends in a swift downward stroke. Write *v* with a sharp point to distinguish it from *u*.

v	save
u	view

Final *gay* and *j*: These end in a swift, solid downward stroke.

g	dog
j	judge

Final *o*: This ends at the top of the circle; *a* ends in a downward stroke.

o	low
a	say

1. Write **o** for the sound of *ow* (ou). Always write this sound in an outline.

allow, a-l-ow	alo	doubt, d-ow-t	dol
now, n-ow	no	out, ow-t	ol
proud, p-r-ow-d	prod	town, t-ow-n	lon

2. Write a printed capital S (joined) for the word beginnings *cer, cir, ser, sur* (pronounced *sir*).

certain, cer-t-n	Sln	serve, ser-v	Sv
survey, sur-v-a	Sva	certificate, cer-t-f-k-t	Slfcl
service, ser-v-s	Svs	sermon, ser-mun	Sm
circle, cir-k-l	Scl	surprise, sur-p-r-z	Sprz

SALUTATIONS

Gentlemen	/	Dear Sir	dS
Ladies	l	Dear Sir or Madam	dS⌒
Ladies and Gentlemen	l/		

PUNCTUATION SYMBOLS

Write ! to indicate an exclamation mark:

What happy news we have for you!

l hpe nz e v f u !

Write = to indicate a hyphen:

Will you recommend a well-known book?

l u rcm . l = nn bc ×

Write ═ to indicate a dash:

We do not know the reason—do you?

e du n no r rzn = du u ×

To indicate solid capitalization, double the curved line underneath the last letter of the outline.

MONEY MANAGEMENT, mun-e manage-ment

To indicate an underlined title, draw a solid line under the outline.

Newsweek, n-z-w-k

PRINCIPLES SUMMARY

1. Write o for the sound of *ow* (ou): allow, a-l-ow alo.
2. Write a printed capital S (joined) for the word beginnings *cer, cir, ser, sur* (sir): certain, cer-t-n Stn.

WORD DEVELOPMENT

Write the shorthand outlines for the following related words.

out ot	-side ______	-line ______	-lines ______
research rSC	-es ______	-ing ______	-er ______
doubt dot	-s ______	-ing ______	-less ______
survey Sva	-s ______	-ing ______	-or ______
allow alo	-s ______	-ing ______	
surprise Sprz	-s ______	-ing ______	

WORD CONSTRUCTION

Practice writing these words.

how, h-ow ______	down, d-ow-n ______
warehouse, w-r-h-ow-s ______	services, ser-v-s-s ______
power, p-ow-r ______	circuit, cir-k-t ______
search, ser-chay ______	outfit, ow-t-f-t ______
outlook, ow-t-l-k ______	serving, ser-v-ing ______
certificates, cer-t-f-k-t-s ______	downtown, d-ow-n-t-ow-n ______

READING AND WRITING EXERCISES

1

2

3

4

s— l sv enf
me f— don pam,
if so e c hlp u.
e r no ofr. nu
h— pam pln
—C l alo u l
pls. lo don pam
o u nu h—. e
aso v. bjl pln
f hos pams. if
u lc ol. ln f—
s no u c scjl
u pams ne —a
u —s, gv s.
ml v u l— +
e l so u. eze
pam pln f u
hoshld. cu

—sn l n prN.
—n / dz prN —
cpes r n clr, e
v —d me cls n
SC v. ajN hu
Svss u —sns.
nn c gl — pls
e nd f rprs,
e hp u c ofr s
. —sn —C gvs
blr Svs. l u ll
s no —l u pln
l du x su

5

1 e r rel — cpe
—sn e bl f— u
fr. s—ds —

6

dS no, — l— l
vzl r sp. e v
. nu lrcld v
h— frnt —C
e r ofr / bq bq
sv l u, dN
dla! vzl s no
+ Cz f— me fn

chs sn o eC	vzl r sp no +
flr, dN fgl=	sv, uvl

LESSON 6

1. To form the past tense of any regular verb, write a hyphen after the outline (pronounced *duh* or *ed*).

used, u-z-duh	uz-	received, re-s-v-duh	rsv-
limited, l-m-t-ed	lmt-	finished, f-n-ish-duh	fns-
helped, h-l-p-duh	hlp-	copied, k-p-e-duh	cpe-

WRITING NUMBERS

Write figures to indicate cardinal numbers.

someone	sm 1	12 pairs	12 prs
anyone	ne 1	two girls	2 grls

ABBREVIATIONS

north	N	west	W
south	S	corporation	corp
east	E	enclose, enclosure	enc

ABBREVIATED WORD DEVELOPMENT

northern	Nrn	eastern	Ern
*southern	Srn	western	Wrn

*Note: Word beginnings and endings may be added to brief forms and abbreviations to form derivatives, even though the pronunciation of the derivative may differ from the root word.

BRIEF FORMS

be, but, been, buy, by b

during du

necessary nes

why y

accept ac

after af

appropriate apo

determine dt

PRINCIPLES SUMMARY

1. To form the past tense of any regular verb, write a hyphen after the outline: used, u-z-duh uz- .

WORD DEVELOPMENT

Write the shorthand outlines for the following related words.

attach atC	-es ______	-ing ______	-ed ______
involve nvlv	-d ______	-s ______	-ment ______
place pls	-ing ______	-d ______	re- ______
apply apli	-ies ______	-ing ______	-ied ______
ask asc	-s ______	-ing ______	-ed ______
agree agre	-d ______	-ing ______	-ment ______

WORD CONSTRUCTION

Practice writing these words.

cashed, k-ish-duh ______

increased, in-k-r-s-duh ______

marked, m-r-k-duh ______

issued, i-ish-u-duh ______

furnished, f-r-n-ish-duh ______

insured, in-ish-r-duh ______

scheduled, s-k-j-l-duh ______

signed, s-n-duh ______

based, b-s-duh ______

informed, in-for-m-duh ______

allowed, a-l-ow-duh ______

amended, a-mend-ed ______

READING AND WRITING EXERCISES

1

d dvd if u r l l
⌒v bc E + ac /
jb v plN ⌒yr /
l b nes f u l sn
/ enc- agrem.
af u rel / agrem
e c dl ⌒n u
dles l bgn, l hp
u l dsd l b . mbr
v r corp. s

2

dS f . l-l- l⌒
e l ofr / ⌒cs
fre vzl l r clys
b / se. if u ac /
l n b nes f u l
pa ne f u r⌒ +
⌒ls, du u vzl
e l so u nu +
uz- ⌒dl clys
⌒C u ⌒a b o r
eze pam pln b
dN dla. y n cl
no + dl . l⌒ f u
fre ⌒c x, e d lc
l so u ho hpe lf
c b / clys b / se.
su

3

dS e cs Ccs f
rzdNs v r lon.
af u v fl-ol /
apo f⌒s u l
rsv . Cc=cs crd
⌒C alos u l cs
Ccs hr / ne l⌒.
e hp l Sv u sn.
vlu

4

d ed enc- , . cpe
v (L u ‿n- l
se , (L Us y /
l b nes l ncrs
(‿l fes + Aso
ho e dl- (ncrss ,
af u v rd (L rel
/ l (apo fl , s

5

dS v rd u artcl
o sl hoss i d
lc l asc u f .
fvr , d u alo s
l rprN u artcl
n r co blln x >
e r Sln ‿l u
sa , bru = (‿r
l gl blr ‿n e
se . ncrs n ln
me , e r U r
ajNs l b psN +
u artcl l hlp > l
u ll s no cf e
c uz / x ru

6

dS i d lc l b . cpe
v u nu bc ho l
ncrs rll sls , af
rd . rsN rvu v
(bc i blv / l
hlp n . cly crs
n ‿C i v nrl ,
bcz clss v bgn i
nd (bc no , cd
u r+ . cpe l ‿i
h‿ adrs gvn n
(abv Lhd x > i
v alC- . Cc l
cvr (prs v (bc
+ ‿l fes , i l b
egr l v u rpli ,
su

LESSON 7

RECAP AND REVIEW

You now know enough shorthand to write most of the words used in business correspondence. This lesson reviews the principles you've studied so far. No new principles will be introduced in this lesson. Instead, use this opportunity to check your progress.

1. The following words illustrate principles you studied in Lessons 1–6:

view, v-u
build, b-l-d
easy, e-z-e

billing, b-l-ing
billings, b-l-ings
something, s-m-thing

member, mem-b-r
money, mun-e
remind, re-mind
settlement, s-t-l-ment

patient, p-ish-nt
engineers, en-j-n-r-s
house, h-ow-s

package, p-k-j
much, m-chay
while, w-l

jobs, j-b-s
Ted's, t-d-s
helps, h-l-p-s

she, ish-e
wish, w-ish
advice, ad-v-s
also, al-s-o

certain, cer-t-n
surplus, sur-p-l-s
copied, k-p-e-duh

2. Following are the brief forms you have studied. Write the outlines for each of these brief forms.

are ________	of ________	is ________
at ________	very ________	for ________
a ________	too ________	in ________
the ________	not ________	us ________
will ________	his ________	full ________
can ________	it ________	have ________
our ________	well ________	to ________
an ________	we ________	from ________
during ________	firm ________	your ________
part ________	perhaps ________	own ________
letter ________	port ________	on ________
market ________	would ________	manage ________
be ________	after ________	buy ________
why ________	but ________	determine ________
by ________	appropriate ________	been ________
accept ________	necessary ________	

3. Write the outlines for these words, which are developed from some of the above brief forms:

haven't ________	yours ________	cancel ________
welfare ________	manager ________	formal ________
report ________	forgotten ________	cannot ________
forgive ________	informing ________	letters ________

4. The following outlines represent the abbreviations you have studied. How quickly can you read them?

co	corp	p
enc	+	vp
inf	ret	E
W	N	S
r	rs	m
s	cal	

READING AND WRITING EXERCISES

1

1 e r hpe u v
dsd- l b u nu co
crs f s, y dN
u vzl s s d
du c c + dl
C dls u
4 l b, e v
me crs C d
b apo f u corp,
r Svs ppl r v
l lrn- + l cp u
crs n lp sp, /
r fr e lc prd n
r Svs + e N
u l b hpe, e r
rde l hlp n
ne a e c, s

2

dS Ph u v fgln u
pam, du, d u
lc . ml l l s
. Cc, e v b psN

b e du n no f u
v rsv- r Ls rm
u l ⌒c u pam o
L. ⌣N u cl s×
/) n nes l pa
u bl n f. f u cn
⌒y l pa / ntr
bl e l ac pl v /)
f / crN pln) l
⌒C f u byl y n
vzl r ln ofs× r
ajN ⌒a b v hlp
l u. uvl

3

d ed enc-) / inf
u ⌣N-. /) . rpl
bs- o . old ⌒r
Sva ⌒d b r VP.
i hp u l fgv /
dla n gl / inf
l u. e cd n gl
/ b / L u ⌣N-

/ bcz v r cpe
⌒sn. / P v r fr
sN / ⌒sn ol
f rprs / s⌒
⌣c e rsv- u L.
e v . co plse
⌣C dz n alo s
l lc fl ⌣ns ol
v / ofs. cu

4

d jl e r gld l
rpl u v b ac-f
clss bgn n / fl.
e rcm u pln
no ⌣l crss u
⌣s l lc. / enc-
cal sd b v hlp)
u ⌒a b Sln /
scls u lrn hr l
b apo f ne ofs.
f u Cz / ⌒dcl
or njnr flds u

lrn l Sv u l,
du fl fre l asc
s f avs / ne
… . e r hpe l
b . pl v u fCr .
su

5

d r Crd no , /
… l pln r
s…r sl . me
rll …yrs hld
lry sls du dfrN
…s v / yr . y
dN e lri s…

nu + dl . … f
i bq s…r evN .
e c lrn / ntr
sp sNr nl .
…yr sd…c sl,
i d lc l se /
sl rn f . f …c .
Ph e cd cp / sps
opn af rglr clz .
…s, f u agre
i l lc l /
…rCNs + ll u
no … l , dsd- .
ul

What Shorthand Will Do for You

Shorthand is a skill that will help launch and then advance your career. Why? Shorthand gives you a special skill that makes you a more versatile employee. Your employer will know that you had the ambition and the ability to learn this skill.

Here are some facts about shorthand and what it can do for you.

Shorthand enables you to begin at higher levels in the business world, which in turn leads to advancement in other areas. You will find that shorthand is helpful at any level—either for taking dictation or giving dictation. Your shorthand will help you get a good job. Advancement from there will depend on your ambition, career goals, and performance.

You can use shorthand in many ways at any job level. Shorthand makes you a more productive employee. Whether you are doing research for a special project, composing a memo or letter, taking notes at a meeting, or recording telephone messages, shorthand saves time and allows faster completion of tasks. Your ability to increase your productivity on the job will help you earn respect as a valuable employee.

*You can learn **Speedwriting Shorthand** quickly. Speedwriting Shorthand* is an alphabetic system of shorthand that can be learned quickly and easily. With more experience on the job, your speed and accuracy will continue to improve.

LESSON 8

1. Write l for the sound of *ith* or *th*.

them, ith-m lm
then, ith-n ln
growth, gay-r-ith grl
health, h-l-ith hll
methods, m-ith-d-s mlds
although, al-ith-o alo

2. Write l for the word ending *ly* or *ily* (pronounced *lee* or *uh-lee*).

family, f-m-ly fml
yearly, y-r-ly yrl
certainly, cer-t-n-ly Stnl
easily, e-z-ly ezl
recently, re-s-nt-ly rsNl
rapidly, r-p-d-ly rpdl

3. Write a capital D for the word beginning *dis*.

discuss, dis-k-s Dcs
display, dis-p-l-a Dpla
dismay, dis-m-a Dma
disturb, dis-t-r-b Dtrb
dislike, dis-l-k Dlc
distant, dis-t-nt DtN

4. Write a capital M for the word beginning *mis*.

mistake, mis-t-k Mlc

mislay, mis-l-a Mla

mislead, mis-l-d Mld

misfit, mis-f-t Mfl

misplaced, mis-p-l-s-duh Mpls-

misgivings, mis-gay-v-ings Mgv=

Word beginnings, word endings, and sound blends that can also be individual words can be used to express those words.

add a

missing M̲

all a

*men m

*Remember that *man* is written ⁀m.

Read and practice these additional words. Each word will be used in the Reading and Writing Exercises at the end of this lesson.

discover, dis-k-v-r Dcvr

either, e-ith-r elr

evidently, e-v-d-nt-ly evdNl

these, ith-z lz

really, r-l-ly rll

this, ith-s ls

nearly, n-r-ly nrl

there, their, ith-r lr

gladly, gay-l-d-ly gldl

misprint, mis-p-r-nt MprN

BRIEF FORM DEVELOPMENT

Use the principles you have learned in this lesson to develop new outlines from brief forms.

necessarily nesl

reportedly rpl-l

appropriately apol

willingly l̲l

partly pll

firmly frl

YOUR BUSINESS VOCABULARY

When you begin your office career, you will learn many words that are commonly used in business offices. Some you may already know. Others will become familiar as you use them. The following words will appear in the Reading and Writing Exercises at the end of this lesson. Make these words part of your business vocabulary.

marketing — Those activities involved in getting a product from the producer to the consumer, such as advertising, promoting, and selling.

yearly report *yrl rpl* — A summation of the activities of a department, division, or entire corporation over a 12-month period.

PRINCIPLES SUMMARY

1. Write *l* for the sound of *ith* or *th*: them, ith-m *lm*; growth, gay-r-ith *grl*.
2. Write *l* for the word ending *ly* (lee) or *ily* (uh-lee): family, f-m-ly *fml*.
3. Write a capital *D* for the word beginning *dis*: discuss, dis-k-s *Dcs*.
4. Write a capital *M* for the word beginning *mis*: mistake, mis-t-k *Mtc*.

WORD DEVELOPMENT

Write the shorthand outlines for the following related words.

play *pla* dis- ______ -ed ______ -ing ______

short *Srl* -s ______ -ly ______ -age ______

take *tc* mis- ______ -s ______ -ing ______

clear *clr* -ly ______ -ed ______ -ing ______

time *lm* -d ______ -ing ______ -ly ______

WORD CONSTRUCTION

Practice writing these words.

therefore, ith-r-for ______ mistaken, mis-t-k-n ______

through, ith-r-u ______ only, on-ly ______

whether, w-ith-r ________ disclose, dis-k-l-z ________

misprints, mis-p-r-nt-s ________ than, ith-n ________

accordingly, a-k-r-d-ing-ly ________ discussed, dis-k-s-duh ________

WRITING ASSIGNMENT

Write the following sentences in shorthand.

1. Do you have plans for retirement? We have a new policy which pays very well.
2. The agent sent us a memo reminding us to mail our payment.
3. We are paying too much money for the policy. May we look for a new agent?
4. We could file a new claim. We will let you know if we reach a settlement.
5. We are seeing a high demand for the new policy.

READING AND WRITING EXERCISES

1

mo l bb s-d / ,
nsl L f r f-d
c-p l bgn, e v
n hrd f- a r
f-ls, l u cl +
rm L l fl ol
Ls hll f-s, r
f-s c b -l- l
s, e rll nd r
f-s bf c-p opns,

2

mo l a co -yrs
alC- r r n-s v
M fls, aprMl r
fls v b Mpls-, d
eC v u lc lru u
pprs l se y r M
fls cd v b Mla-

o u dsc x > me v r
fldrs r old + v
mld Uls . ls Mlcs
c ezl b d .

3

drs lsn i
nl U u ho
C i lc nu
hll fd Dplas u
v n u fr se . / /
ncy l se grl
n hll fds n ls
sle . i U u d lc
l se enc-
artcl C Dcss
s rzns e r
se sC . rpd Cny
n hll fd r .
Ph / l ncy u l
cp A l u Dpla .
s

4

dS rsNl i bl 2
lvl Crs f u
co . Alo Crs
v b uz- f . flr
Dpla nlr so-
ne dy / c b .
n Crs arv-
/ i h i fll
v Dlrb- . l
Da i Dcvr- .
rlr lry rp n
fbrc . elr i dd
n se rp n
i bl Crs or /
hpn- dy lrp l
i hos . n elr
cs Crs l v l
b rel- . s

5

mo l A r hds

n u yrl rpl l u
Dcs s— nu
—lds v —r r
nu nyns, e r
pln l sl hi gls
f sls ls yr +
nd —as l hlp
s aCv l—. Ph
u cd gv s / rzlts

v u rsM —r
rSC n —C u
asc- dlrs f lr
vus o fCr sls.
/ —a b nes l
dl . nu plse l
b uz-n r co. if
so u rpl d Stnl
b v hlp.

LESSON

1. Retain beginning or ending vowels when building compound words.

When you combine two words to make one word, you are building a compound word. If one of these words begins or ends in a vowel, keep the vowel in the outline: payroll = pay + roll *parl* .

headachе, h-d + a-k *hdac* | teenage, t-n + a-j *tnaj*

seaside, s-e + s-d *sesd* | highway, h-i + w-a *hia*

2. Retain the first and final root-word vowel when adding prefixes and suffixes. When a prefix contains a long vowel followed by a root-word vowel, omit the prefix vowel.

disappear, dis-a-p-r *Dapr* | misuse, mis-u-z *Muz*

payment, p-a-ment *pam* | disallow, dis-a-l-ow *Dalo*

reapply, re-a-p-l-i *rapli* | readmit, re-ad-m-t *rA—t*

MORE ABOUT NUMBERS

An ordinal number shows the sequence of an item in a set: *third* child, *fifth* day. Write ordinal numbers in the following way:

42nd *42 d* | 53rd *53 d*

85th *85 t*

ABBREVIATIONS

credit cr

total tot

amount a-t

number No

percent %

attention att

BRIEF FORMS

as, was z

hospital hsp

general jn

arrange ar

great, grate gr

were, with ‿

that ta

BRIEF FORM DEVELOPMENT

Use your new brief forms to develop other outlines.

within ‿n

greatly grl

arrangements arms

generally jnl

without ‿ol

YOUR BUSINESS VOCABULARY

reassess rass — To re-evaluate, or to determine a new value of property as a basis for taxation.

minimum payment mm pam — The least amount of money required at specific dates on a credit purchase.

PRINCIPLES SUMMARY

1. Retain beginning and ending vowels when building compound words: payroll = pay + roll parl .
2. Retain the initial and final root-word vowel when adding prefixes and suffixes: reopen, re-o-p-n ropn ; payment, p-a-ment pam .

WORD DEVELOPMENT

Write the shorthand outlines for the following related words.

amount a-t -s ________ -ed ________ -ing ________

number No -s ________ -ed ________ -ing ________

total *lol*	-s ________	-ed ________	-ing ________
any *ne*	-how ________	-where ________	-way ________
apply *apli*	re- ________	-ies ________	-ing ________

WORD CONSTRUCTION

Practice writing these words.

arranged, arrange-duh ________	lower, l-o-r ________
herewith, h-r-with ________	payroll, p-a-r-l ________
higher, h-i-r ________	greater, great-r ________
highly, h-i-ly ________	lowering, l-o-r-ing ________
throughout, ith-r-u-ow-t ________	photograph, f-t-o-gay-r-f ________

WRITING ASSIGNMENT

Write the following sentences in shorthand.

1. We recommend using our new checks.
2. We will print new checks for you. Do you want us to mail the checks to you at home?
3. You will have to pay a minimum fee and make a deposit if you want to use our new checks.
4. The president wants a copy sent to each of the board members.
5. The desk clerk will return the deposit to you.

READING AND WRITING EXERCISES

1

mo l a cls | *yrs z hd v ls*

| *corp l z v hpe*

l lrn l . gr jb
u r a du . No v
ppl v rln l sa
la lr cls gvn
v fn all . ol .
dol a v u dzrv
cr f u pl n gv ls
co . gr n .

2

dS pa bls c n
hdac af hdac .
la , y e r ofr .
nu cr pln .
ls pln u pa , lol
a l . ln e uz la
a l l pa a v c
bls u o , f u bls
r lc l C c+
f u bjl ll s
ar . eze pln f u .
n . yr u bls l
b pd + u hdac

l b gn . su

3

p e rsv- u L nf
s la r sesd cly l
b rass- o c 14 l .
c L N o l sa
la c vlu v ls
hos ncrs- grl=
b 25%= n c nu
h a z bll , e r
sre b u v d .
Mlc . c h a
C rns nr r
bC hos , n nu .
f ne c , old +
bdl n nd v rpr .
c h a z bll . fu
yrs af e bl r
bC hos . l r nly
c rd z nvr rpr-
af c z bll , e hp
la u ofs l lc . blr

lc / la hea. if r
hos, rass-e d
lc l se apo rprs
—d o r rd. vlu

nu l rpl. e r
hpe l v b v hlp.
vlu

4

d—r —lr e dd Cc
l se if u l rsv
u crs o scyl. e
cl- r lrc fr l dl
—n r crs d arv
n nu hvn + r
—yr sd r crs
lft erl ls —rn.
Alo s— v r lrcs
r b dla- us sd
arv o h ls —c.
r —yr asr- s u l
gl . cl if ls , ne

5

d lu r rsv- . L f—
r bron + a—s lrc
fr asc f . cpe v
r yrl agrem. i
v lc- n a v r fl
cbnls b i v n
sn r agrem.
cd / v b Mpls-x
lr r 2 fls —C sd
v . cpe v r agrem.
eC cpe s—s l
b M. i hp u
c Avz —e o ho
l gl . cpe. ul

LESSON 10

1. Write a capital *P* (disjoined from other letters) for the word beginnings *per* and *pur*.

person, per-s-n Psn

personnel, per-s-n-l Psnl

permit, per-m-t P-t

per P

purchase, pur-chay-s PCs

purpose, pur-p-s Pps

Write a capital *P* also for the word beginnings *pre, pro,* and *pro* pronounced as *prah*.

prefer, pre-f-r Pfr

problem, prah-b-l-m Pbl

provide, pro-v-d Pvd

proper, prah-p-r Ppr

proposal, pro-p-z-l Ppzl

produce, pro-d-s Pds

2. Write *q* for the word ending *gram*.

program, pro-gram Pq

telegram, t-l-gram tlq

YOUR BUSINESS VOCABULARY

proposal Ppzl — A plan of action, usually presented in writing.

out-patients — Patients receiving treatment at a hospital without being admitted for overnight stays.

building permit — A legal document authorizing an organization or individual to begin construction of a building.

PRINCIPLES SUMMARY

1. Write a disjoined capital P for the word beginnings *per, pur, pre, pro,* and *pro* (prah): person, per-s-n ; prepare, pre-p-r ; produce, pro-d-s ; problem, prah-b-l-m .
2. Write g for the word ending gram: program, pro-gram .

WORD DEVELOPMENT

Write the shorthand outlines for the following related words.

purchase	-ing ______	-d ______	-s ______
proceed	-s ______	-ing ______	-ed ______
produce	re- ______	-ing ______	-s ______
profit	-s ______	-ed ______	-ing ______
progress	-ed ______	-ing ______	-ive ______

WORD CONSTRUCTION

Practice writing these words.

programs, pro-gram-s ______ procedure, pro-s-j-r ______

prepared, pre-p-r-duh ______ telegrams, t-l-gram-s ______

purposes, pur-p-s-s ______ providing, pro-v-d-ing ______

personally, per-s-n-l-ly ______ process, prah-s-s ______

problems,
prah-b-l-m-s ________

proposed,
pro-p-z-duh ________

Write the following sentences in shorthand.

WRITING ASSIGNMENT

1. We will admit you to the hospital as soon as we can arrange it.
2. We are increasing the amount of your credit. The new total of your loan is shown below.
3. We are offering this chair at 20 percent less than the regular price.
4. Did you know that a great number of teenage drivers are insured with our firm?
5. In general, the training class went well even though there was a great deal of disagreement.

READING AND WRITING EXERCISES

1

mo l gr v PCs
l , r crM
plse o PCs ofs
splis. C cos
v alo- s cr. du
e nd . cr crd
l c . PCs or c
e Pvd r ofs No.,
aso l , r m
v r Psn hu
asns cr crds.
l hp u c Pvd
e ls inf.
/ l b . gr hlp l
lrn r Ppr PCs
lds.

2

mo l a Psnl enc-
) . cpe v r nu
Ppzl. z u c se

i Pvds me nd-
Cnjs. — ls pln
eC Psn l rsv dl
bnfts —ol pa f
(ncrs- cvrj.
Psnll i blv ls
pln , —l e v
nd- f me yrs.
i se no Pbl—s
— // A, e r
Aso rvz r plse
f lrn nu Psnl.
szn jns , Ppr.
mo —C l Pvd
A (dlls. i blv
la lz nu plses
l slv me Pbl—s
n (co.

l Pvd . dzn f (
bld z l z jn inf
nd- l gl . bld
P—l. y dN u Ppr
. nz rls gv dlls
v (Ppzl? rzdNs
v ls sle Ad no la
r hsp l ofr me
nu Pgs —C l
bnfl ol=pANs z
l z n=pANs,
e v rsv- —C
all f— (nzppr
rsNl du l ncrs-
hsp fes. ls d s—
l b . apo L— l
ll ppl no r plns
l ncrs Svss.

3

mo l —r rbrl
L—pl n —i Ppzl
f (nu hsp i pln

4

mo l j—s bron
—l , u Avs o (
alC- hll cr Pq?

ls Pq r co d
Pvd . pls z l z .
f rn or s .
/ z Ppz- la e uz
r S sd v r bld
f ls Pps, ls pln
z Ppz- b r P hu
blvs la ppl sd
b alo- l gl Ppr
hll cr l o lr
jbs, du u se
ne Pbl s sC
. arm.

5

1 r Pps v ls L , l
dl y e v n rsv-
r crds e PCs-f

u co, n e dsd-
l b r crds u
Sln la e d v
ahd v , z l
rcl e asc- la r
crds b rs-, u
ayN asr- s la lr
d b no Pbl du
ls v r yr, e v
b psN b 3 cs v
gn b + e v n
rsv- r crds, e
hp la / l n b nes
l csl b af ls c
e l n ac r crds.
f no o d b apo
f u l nf s v
dlas b Uq, ul

LESSON 11

1. Write y for the sound of *oi* (oy). Always write this sound in an outline.

boy, b-oi by

choice, chay-oi-s Cys

join, j-oi-n jyn

loyal, l-oi-l lyl

voice, v-oi-s vys

annoy, a-n-oi any

WRITING MONTHS

Write the months of the year in the following way:

January Ja

February Fb

March Mr

April Ap

May Ma

June Jn

July Jl

August Ag

September Sp

October Oc

November Nv

December Dc

ABBREVIATIONS

department dpt

envelope env

invoice inv

insurance ins

regard re

BRIEF FORMS

between	bln	participate	pp
ship	A	property	prp
situate	sil	refer	rf
those	loz	respond, response	rsp
operate	op	suggest	sug
point	py		

BRIEF FORM DEVELOPMENT

leadership	ldrA	situated	sil-
operator	opr	shipment	Am
appointment	apym	disappoint	Dapy

PRINCIPLES SUMMARY

1. Write y for the sound of *oi* (oy): boy, b-oi by .

WORD DEVELOPMENT

Write the shorthand outlines for the following related words.

point py	ap- ____	-ed ____	-s ____
avoid avyd	-s ____	-ed ____	-ing ____
regard re-	-s ____	dis- ____	-ing ____
join jyn	-ed ____	-s ____	-ing ____
member mbr	-s ____	-ship ____	-ships ____

WORD CONSTRUCTION

Practice writing these words.

soil, s-oi-l ____ suggested, suggest-ed ____

enjoyed, en-j-oi-duh ____ shipments, ship-ment-s ____

noise, n-oi-z ________ joint, j-oi-nt ________

oil, oi-l ________ referred, refer-duh ________

joy, j-oi ________ responding, respond-ing ________

WRITING ASSIGNMENT

Write the following sentences in shorthand.

1. The total amount was due by the 12th. Your attention to this matter would be a great help.
2. There were as many men as there were women in the total number of people on the payroll.
3. You will receive your new credit card without delay.
4. As soon as the matter was brought to my attention, I asked that new arrangements be made.
5. We were happy to learn that sales are generally doing very well in the East.

READING AND WRITING EXERCISES

1

1 n u L v Ap 13 u
rf- l . dla n r Ja
sm v ofs splis.
e r sre f ne Pbls
cz- b r dla b r cpe
v r inv sos la u
splis — s- 3 sn
3 pam 3 rsv-.

—a e sug ls —ld
f gl u sm v envs
o L, u c avyd
dla b —l u Cc b
Ma 30. u envs l
b s- o Jn 7 or r
flo —c, f u flo
ls pln f fCr PCss
e c Pvd u — blr

Svs, su

2

djsn u rsN apym
z VP z gr nz, ⌒ co
Slnl ⌒d. ⌒z Cys,
z hd v ⌒ A dpl u
Pvd- me yrs v lyl
Svs, / , rasr l
se ⌒ co rsp b gv
u Ppr cr, ⌒ u ldrs
a dpls l no op
efsNl, l hp u l
cl o ⌒e l hlp n
ne ⌒a l c, z sn
z u v s⌒ fre ⌒
y dN e gl lglr f
lnC. vlu

3

dS dd u no la u
⌒a b pa bln 15 +
20% l ⌒c f u ins.
dd u Aso no la
loz plses ⌒a n
cvr ⌒ crN vlu
v u h⌒ + Psnl
prp., no , ⌒ ⌒
l ⌒c Sln la u
bnfls r a la u sd
v, bln Mr 15 + Ap1
r ajN l cl o u, y
n ⌒c / . py l v
u plses rde f rvu.
cu

4

mo l VP folr n
re l u mo v Sp 5
⌒ prN ⌒ns l b
sil- n r plN b ⌒
bgn v Dc, z u no
e ⌒N- l v ⌒ rde
erl n Oc b cd n
ar l v ⌒ A- / la
⌒, e v asc- . lol

v 30 ~sn oprs l
pp n . lrn Pq du
Nv b e v n rsv-
rsps f~ a v h~>
Ph e sd pln l hr
nu ppl l op ~ ~sns.
~l du u sug x

5

mo l frd gra ι c
no gv u r nu plse
f nsr ~sns s- b
lrc. l u nf~ a pp
dlrs la bgn Jl ι e
l n rpls ~sns
dy- o ~ dlrs prp x
if ~ dlrs ~s l Dcs
ls ~lr rf h~ l ~
cl~s dpl> e asc
la ne dy b sn o
~ inv / ~ py v
arvl> e d lc ~
dlrs l b lld v ~
Cnys no. ~n. fu
~cs Ls l b ~l-
gv f dlls v ~ nu
plse.

LESSON 12

1. For words ending in a long vowel + *t* (*ate, ete, ite, ote, ute/oot*), omit the *t* and write the vowel.

rate, r-ate	right, write, r-ite
late, l-ate	might, m-ite
meet, m-ete	wrote, r-ote
beat, b-ete	boat, b-ote
cute, k-ute	suit, s-oot

Write these additional words that are used in the Reading and Writing Exercises at the end of this lesson.

locate, l-k-ate	invite, in-v-ite
hesitate, h-z-t-ate	receipt, re-s-ete
defeated, d-f-ete-ed	promoted, pro-m-ote-ed
delighted, d-l-ite-ed	white, w-ite
vote, v-ote	fight, f-ite

REVIEWING PROPER NAMES

You have already learned how to write proper names. As a brief review exercise, write the following names. Each name is written according to the principles you have learned.

Janet, j-n-t

William, w-l-y-m

Pamela, p-m-l-a

David, d-v-d

Elizabeth, e-l-z-b-ith

Ronald, r-n-l-d

Claire, k-l-r

Martin, m-r-t-n

Shelley, ish-l-e

Jim, j-m

Barbara, b-r-b-r-a

Jeremy, j-r-m-e

PRINCIPLES SUMMARY

1. For words ending in a long vowel + *t*, omit the *t* and write the vowel: rate, r-ate .

WORD DEVELOPMENT

Write the shorthand outlines for the following related words.

date	-s ______	-ing ______	-d ______
duplicate	-ing ______	-d ______	-s ______
meet	-s ______	-ing ______	-ings ______
separate	-s ______	-d ______	-ing ______
locate	-ing ______	-d ______	-s ______

WORD CONSTRUCTION

Practice writing these words.

freight, f-r-ate ______

site, s-ite ______

sheet, ish-ete ______

united, u-n-ite-ed ______

writing, r-ite-ing ______

treatment, t-r-ete-ment ______

light, l-ite ______

related, re-l-ate-ed ______

regulate, r-gay-l-ate ______

eliminate, e-l-min-ate ______

WRITING ASSIGNMENT

Write the following sentences in shorthand.

1. Although we have no jobs open at this time, we advise you to reapply when the new hospital opens. We will make arrangements to discuss your letter at that time.
2. We will add a total of 20 new men to the payroll. We will need that many to help build the new highway.
3. As a rule, our company does not lay off people. Rather than release men and women from their jobs, we reassign them to new duties. I believe that we will reassign a great number this year.
4. In general, our company offers better benefits than any large firm in town. I have been with this corporation for 11 years now, and I know that this is true.
5. We will be happy to readmit you in our classes. You will receive full credit for the courses you took earlier.

READING AND WRITING EXERCISES

1

2

+ bgn dcra ~r
nu ofss, u L lls
~e la . rse f ~ pN
z enc-, ~ rse z n
n ~ L, ~l sl i
du., l i nd ~ rse
~n i gl ~ pN. f
so l u ~l ~e .
cpe ri a~a., cl
~e f lr , ne i
nd l du, uvl

3

d edlr brns e ~
dli- ~ ~ gr cvry
u gv r fl crnvl,
e cd n v hp- f .
blr rsp ln e rsv-,
e r no nvi u l pp
n . evN e v b pln
f 2 yrs, ls evN l
b cl- ~ vlj bo so,
~ bos l b Dpla-
n r vlj sp sNr,
ri no / lcs z lo
e ~a v s~ rlr
lry bos hr, f nes
loz bos l b lca- n
~ E prc ll, e r
pln l v bln 20 +
30 bos o Dpla f
1 ~c n Ap, l u
pln l ri . arlcl l
rn du ~ ~c v ~
so. e Aso sug rn
. arlcl s~ la n
Mr, i fl Sln la i
cd ar . Pvu v ~
bos f la d hlp, y
dN e ~e f lnCl
Dcs ~as v P~o ~
so. s

4

dS enc-, u Jn bl,
f u pa ~ lol a~l

b r da sn o r bl
u l sv me. flo la
da . 5% fe l b a-l
u bl, / d b ~z l
avryd la pams. if
u du da , . Pbl u
~ ~s l Dcs nu
bl das ~ r cr ~yr.
if u cl f . apym r
~yr l b hpe l pln
. ~e L . s

5

mo l VP rbrls e
~ a Sprz- l lrn
la P ~ rzn- ,

ofs af r brd ~e.
z u no , Ppzl z
dfe- b . vo v 8 L 4.
evdNl r brds vo
z . dp Psnl Dapym,
e a fl sre la r P
fll / nes l rzn.
~C v ls cos grl
z rla- l , ldrs. e
hp r P l dsd l
rm ~ ls corp.
/ ~ hlp if u d
ru . L asc P ~
l ~e ~ r brd ls
~c. Ph / , n l la
l Cny , m o ls ~dr.

LESSON 13

1. Write *a* for the word beginning *an*.

answer, an-s-r *asr*

antique, an-t-k *alc*

anticipate, an-t-s-p-ate *alspa*

analyze, an-l-z *alz*

2. Write *q* for the medial or final sound of any vowel + *nk* (*ank, enk, ink, onk, unk*).

bank, b-ank *bq*

blank, b-l-ank *blq*

thank, ith-ank *lq*

length, l-enk-ith *lql*

rank, r-ank *rq*

link, l-ink *lq*

ABBREVIATIONS

junior *jr*

senior *sr*

second, secretary *sec*

BRIEF FORMS

am, more ⌒

charge *C*

doctor, direct *dr*

go, good *g*

he, had, him *h*

they *ly*

PHRASING

Some word combinations, such as *we are* and *to be*, are used so often that they are usually spoken and read as a group. In shorthand, take advantage of this natural association by joining words together in one outline. This practice is called *phrasing*.

we are	to be

The pronouns *I*, *we*, and *you* followed by a verb and the word *to* followed by a verb can be easily written and recognized as phrases.

I am	you are
I can	you can
we are	to be
we can	to go

With experience in taking dictation, phrases will occur to you naturally as you write. The context, or meaning, of the sentence will help you read the phrase correctly when you see it in your notes.

The following phrases will be used in the Reading and Writing Exercises in this and following lessons:

I am	you are
I can	you can
I had	you have
I have	you know
I will	you will
I will be	you would
we are	to be
we can	to go
we have	to have
we hope	to have you

we would *ed*
we would be *edb*
to have your *lvu*
to know *lno*
to pay *lpa*

WRITING CONTRACTIONS

When writing contractions that might be read back as a phrase, use an apostrophe to avoid confusion.

I will *il*
I'll *i'l*
you will *ul*
you'll *u'l*
we are *er*
we're *e'r*

HIGH-FREQUENCY PHRASES

A few word combinations occur together so frequently that certain words within the combinations may be omitted from your shorthand notes. Three such high-frequency phrases are *thank you for, thank you for your,* and *thank you for your letter.* In the following examples, the italicized words have been omitted in the shorthand outlines.

thank *you* for *lqf*
thank *you* for *your* *lqf*
thank *you* for *your* letter *lqfL*

PRINCIPLES SUMMARY

1. Write *a* for the word beginning *an*: answer, an-s-r *asr*.
2. Write *q* for the medial or final sound of any vowel + *nk*: bank, b-ank *bq*.

WORD DEVELOPMENT

Write the shorthand outlines for the following related words.

bank *bq*	-s ________	-ed ________	-ing ________
link *lq*	-s ________	-ed ________	-ing ________
length *lql*	-s ________	-en ________	-ening ________

analyze *alz* -d ______ -ing ______ -s ______

anticipate *alspa* -s ______ -d ______ -ing ______

WORD CONSTRUCTION

Practice writing these words.

thinking, ith-ink-ing ______

thanks, ith-ank-s ______

ago, a-go ______

directly, direct-ly ______

answering, an-s-r-ing ______

charges, charge-s ______

you're, u-'-r ______

anxious, a-ank-ish-s ______

we'll, we-'-l ______

going, go-ing ______

WRITING ASSIGNMENT

Write the following sentences in shorthand.

1. Our new offices will be situated on the property between our main plant and the old office building.
2. Our plant will not operate between January 28 and February 15. We will use those weeks to situate furnishings in the new building. All of our people will participate in the move.
3. During those weeks, we suggest that all shipments be referred to our main plant. All invoices should be referred to our shipping department.
4. In regard to your recent memo, our move will be covered by insurance. A copy of our policy is enclosed in the attached envelope.
5. Can you suggest changes in this schedule? When may I have your response to these plans?

READING AND WRITING EXERCISES

Watch for phrases beginning with the words *I*, *we*, *you*, and *to*.

1

f ls sle, l ev
l rpls ⌢ ⌢sns.
er hp la uc hlp
s avyd du la,
nu ⌢sns sl f.
hi prs ⌣l r uz-
⌢sns r ⌣rl lll
⌢ ln jq, r ⌢r
⌢yr, pln lb n
sn frnssco v sn,
cd u ⌢e ⌣h. cu

bss e s⌣ls v. fu
pl=l opn f hi scl
jrs + srs, bl gra
, . sr hu, fns,
sec yr ⌣ r fr, l
sug la u lc ⌣h,
uc Aso gl ⌢ inf
f r Psnl ⌢yr ⌢rc
lc, if u cn se h Psnll
, sec l gv u ⌢ apo
frs l fl ol, vlu

2

dM adrsn lqf L
re jbs f hi scl
srs, u grds du
ndd rq u / ⌢ lp
v u cls, edb gld
lvu apli, ⌢ enc
. co blln ⌣C l
spli me v ⌢ asrs
u nd, Alo jnl e
nd secs o . f=l

3

ds ⌢lr ⌢ rel
⌢ blg Cc u sN s
b Mlc, ehp la ul
⌢ls . sec Cc ⌣ol
dla, bcz uv . q cr
rq ul n b C- . la fe,
ed lc l sug la u
uz r prN-envs f
⌢l u pams, loz
envs r adrs-l ⌢

cr dpl + u pams
l b sN drl l ⌐ Ppr
ofs, lqf gv̲ ls ⌒dr
u all. ul

4

d bb lqf Avs o ⌐
frq̆ nlsn cs. frq̆
l b gld lno la . sr
mbr v ⌐ fr, l̲ lq
l bl f h. frq̆ + ι v
h enf ⌐ l Ďcs,
Pbl ⌐ lql. Alo h
dz n alspa rsv̲,
old rq frq̆ blvs la
. gr No v ppl l bnfl
f h ⌣ns ls cs. ι
lq h, ri + ér hp̲ ⌐
jj lqs so l, íl Snl
ll uno f uc hlp.
cu

5

ddr a⌐s ι ⌣N u
lno la ⌐ lc̲ f
⌒ alc frn+̲ f u
ofs. ⌣ lca- . dsc
+ Cr ⌣C ι lq ul
lc b ⌐ afrd la
⌐ lql v ⌐ dsc,
n ri f u ofs. ⌣l
d b . q ⌐ f u l lc
/ / ×, ι Aso no v
. ns alc dsc f u
sec. íl lv ⌐ li
oc fn+. ι lq ⌐ d
b ⌒ apo f u ⌣a̲
r⌐ ln f u ofs. e
⌒ι v ι Pbl. ⌐
+p ⌒gr, Cq̲ . gr
dl ⌒ ln u ⌒a +
lpa. Ph ec gl h l
lc ls. ll ⌒e no
⌣n ιc +o u lz fn
alcs. su

LESSON 14

RECAP AND REVIEW

1. Here are the word beginnings you studied in Lessons 8–13:

dis D
mis M
per, pur P
an a
pre, pro, pro *(prah)* P

2. The following word endings were also presented:

long vowel + t
ly l
ate a
gram g
ete e
ite i
ote o
ute/oot u

3. The following words illustrate all of the principles you studied in Lessons 8–13:

dismay, dis-m-a Dma
person, per-s-n Psn
mistake, mis-t-k Mtc
purpose, pur-p-s Pps
recently, re-s-nt-ly rsNl
prevent, pre-v-nt PvN
rate, r-ate ra
program, pro-gram Pg
health, h-l-ith hli
loyal, l-oi-l lyl

reapply, re-a-p-l-i *rapli*

payroll, p-a-r-l *parl*

answer, an-s-r *asr*

bank, b-ank *bq*

4. Months of the year are written this way:

January	*Ja*	July	*Jl*
February	*Fb*	August	*Aq*
March	*Mr*	September	*Sp*
April	*Ap*	October	*Oc*
May	*Ma*	November	*Nv*
June	*Jn*	December	*Dc*

5. Can you automatically write these brief forms? If you are unsure of any brief form, practice the outline until you can write it without hesitation.

that ______	arrange ______	were ______
participate ______	between ______	ship ______
response ______	great ______	as ______
was ______	with ______	hospital ______
those ______	situate ______	general ______
refer ______	property ______	operate ______
respond ______	suggest ______	am ______
more ______	direct ______	doctor ______
charge ______	go ______	he ______
good ______	had ______	they ______
him ______	point ______	

6. Write these brief form derivatives.

arrangement ________	generally ________	operators ________
within ________	without ________	wasn't ________
greatly ________	referred ________	shipping ________

7. How quickly can you read the following abbreviations?

cr	No	ins
re	all	a—d
%	env	dpl
inv	lol	jr
sr	sec	

READING AND WRITING EXERCISES

1

dr bron / dlus —e l nf— u la r cr dpl agre- l r lol a—d v u ln. ec Aso ar f. don pam v bln 12 + 15 % , u ln z rf- l r cr —jr + / rsv- cls all. z u —a no er v Pbl—s gl prp lns lru. / z. hlp la u prp , lca- nr r nu hsp. la As. gr dl l r vlu v u prp , d u rel r enc- agrem n r env

Pvd-x e l nd u
rsp b Fb 10. su

2

mo l A Psnl hr ,
gr nz f loz v u hu
lc- r old hll pln.
ul lv r nu 1, bgn
Ag 15 e l ofr . nu
plse C l Pvd me
v r bnfls uv b asc
f. / l pa z C z
80% v r lol hsp
bl. / Aso pas dcl
fes + Pvds dNl cvry
z l, ls pln uc
ar f r ins co lpa u
dcl bls f u. lr l
b no nd f u l ri .
Cc v u o. ls Svs l
sv + me f u,
loz v u l lrn

r dlls v ls pln l
b nvi-l Dcs / n
. e / r ofs.

3

d szn e l sn b op
nu ldrs. rsNl
r brd vo- l apy .
nu P. . No v ms
sug-. . ofr z d
ri a a b r Psn
Czn dd n ac, / ls
L ic sa la e nvi-
. v fn Psn l ac r
ofr + se rsp- l l
/. hr m l b gvn
/ r brd e o Oc 4.
ehp la A brd mbrs
l b lr l pp. l u c
arms f s, Ub lr
f eC v r dpls. ul

4

dr evns ls , n
rsp l u L U s y
e dd n rsv , Ja
sm . w Dcs- ,
Pbl ppl +
c no U u l hpn-
e dd v s , o dle ,
, h , sm arv-
b , sm z n brl l
, ri pls, n , fCr
d u nf u brc fr
la a sms sd arv
, , rsv dc o , E
sd v r bld. e l
b Sln lv . Psn lr ,
a hs l sn , inv
+ ac , sm . vlu

5

d bl ch . q e
dr s . h lqs e
sd PCs , dl
S80 unl . , Pvds
. dr lq bln , opr
+ , sNrl mre
bq . ls , . nu Pq
C c b ofr- , .
mm C, dr s
fls la . sec unl
d alo s l op evn
efsNl . il b gld
lvu avs, du u alspa
q l , e n ls vgs.
ilb lr if ic gl . dr
fli f dnvz . vlu

The Importance of Listening

Among the many skills that can help make you successful, listening is one of the most essential. Effective listening increases your productivity by helping you understand the needs, desires, and ideas of the persons you work with. It helps you respond more quickly and efficiently and reduces the amount of time that you spend solving problems.

Effective listening differs from hearing. Listening is an active process. Good listeners do not just sit and let listening happen. They participate in the communication process by focusing on what the speaker is saying and thinking about how they will respond.

Some guidelines for becoming a better listener include the following:

1. Show interest in what the speaker is saying by maintaining eye contact.
2. Keep your attention focused on the speaker. When your thoughts start to drift or when you begin to daydream, immediately concentrate on the speaker again.
3. Search for the speaker's thoughts and ideas rather than focusing on just the speaker's words.
4. Summarize the speaker's message or theme, separate the major points from the minor ones, and remember the specific facts that support the theme.

The ability to recognize and summarize major ideas is especially important when you combine your listening skills and shorthand skills to record dictation. On the job, shorthand can be used to record the dictation of letters and memos, to record instructions from a supervisor, to record information from telephone messages, to write instructions for work assignments, to make personal notes, and to record minutes and other information at meetings.

When you take dictation, focus your attention on the dictator even more sharply than you would in notetaking so that you can hear and accurately record every word. However, if you miss a word, skip a space and ask the dictator to repeat it for you immediately after the dictation.

Effective listening is vital not only to developing your shorthand skill, but also to making you a productive and valuable employee.

LESSON 15

1. Write a printed capital S (disjoined) for the word beginning *super*.

supervise, super-v-z Svz

superman, super-m-n S‿m

supermarket, super-market S‿r

supersonic, super-s-n-k Ssnc

superpower, super-p-ow-r Spor

supervisor, super-v-z-r Svzr

2. Write a printed capital S (disjoined) also for the word endings *scribe* and *script* and for the sound of *scrip*.

describe, d-scribe dS

inscribe, in-scribe nS

described, d-scribe-duh dS-

script S

prescribe, pre-scribe PS

*manuscripts, m-n-script-s ‿mSs

*A disjoined word ending is disjoined from the letters that precede it, not from those that follow it.

3. Write el for the word beginning *electr*.

electric, electr-k	elc	electrical, electr-k-l	elcl
electronic, electr-n-k	elnc	electronically, electr-n-k-ly	elncl

MORE ABOUT PHRASES

In Lesson 13, you learned to write phrases beginning with *I, we, you,* and *to.* You can also write other very common word groups as phrases. The following phrases are among those that appear in the Reading and Writing Exercises in this and following lessons.

I could	icd	will be	lb
I hope	ihp	would be	db
to see	tse	it is	s
for the	f	it's (contraction)	's
of the	v	its (possessive)	s
that you	lau	that your	lau

YOUR BUSINESS VOCABULARY

supermarket chain S-r Cn — A group of large grocery stores owned by the same individual or corporation.

programming Pg- — Providing a computer with programs, which are sets of coded instructions.

PRINCIPLES SUMMARY

1. Write a printed capital S (disjoined) for the word beginning *super*: supervise, super-v-z Svz.
2. Write a printed capital S (disjoined) for the sound of *scrip* and the word endings *scribe* and *script*: describe, d-scribe dS; manuscripts, m-n-script-s -mnSs.
3. Write el for the word beginning *electr*: electric, electr-k elc.

WORD DEVELOPMENT

Write the shorthand outlines for the following related words.

super	S	-vise ______	-vises ______	-vised ______
describe	dS	-s ______	-ing ______	-d ______
inscribe	nS	-s ______	-ing ______	-d ______
electric	elc	-al ______	-ally ______	
electron	eln	-s ______	-ic ______	

WORD CONSTRUCTION

Practice writing these words.

superbowl, super-b-l ______

manuscript, m-n-script ______

prescribing, pre-scribe-ing ______

supersede, super-s-d ______

ascribes, a-scribe-s ______

its, it-s ______

it's, it-'-s ______

supermarkets, super-market-s ______

supervisory, super-v-z-r-e ______

electronics, electr-n-k-s ______

WRITING ASSIGNMENT

Write the following sentences in shorthand.

1. Insuring teenage drivers can be a great headache. Indeed, some parents have called it highway robbery. If you are paying too much to insure your teenage drivers, let GENERAL LIFE help. GENERAL LIFE can insure your teenager for 10 percent less than any large company in town.
2. Here is great news for the head of the family. Our health benefits now pay as much as 90 percent of the total hospital bill. When can we arrange to show you this policy?

3. Attention Policyholders: We are now offering the new dental coverage you have been asking for. You, as well as your family, will benefit greatly from this policy.

4. In response to the increased need, we are opening a central claims department to serve the entire company. Beginning January 2, all claims should be referred to the central claims department. This change will provide an efficient means of processing all claims.

5. My files show that it is now time to review your homeowner's insurance policy. May we get together soon? I will call this week for an appointment.

READING AND WRITING EXERCISES

1

2

d frd dli- lau
Cn v S rs lb jyn
r corp. chp s
evdN ho hpe er
lvu o brd. ur no
pl v fl. ehp lse
u ofn, n u L ac r
ofr u uz- me jnrs
rds l dS i rl.
v gld lv pla-
. pl n lz hpn, z
. er Sln l aCv
me Cnys n ls fr.
s q lno lau lb
Svz Cn. uvl

3

ddr evns dr grn
avz- e la h l n
b lC f s ls fl. z
uno dr grn , .
elcl nynr + hd
v nynr dpl hr. h
, lv r scl l jyn
. lcl fr. z VPh l
Svz elnc Pq f nlr
corp, er hpe f dr
grn b sre lse h
q. h l n b eze l
rpls b corps c pa
elcl nynrs ln
ec, dr grn , ofr l
ri . a dS , jb. i
sug la e pls / n
nynr jrnls +
se l hpns. ul

4

d dvd afrd il
v lb a a f ofs
f . c or so. du
i lrp ol W i
nyr- i bc n . bd
fl. dr PS- dsn
+ . c n bd. hp

la , avs l slv /
Pbl . f / dz n /
dr a v l op. /
d ln b nes f e
l lc . dcl lv v
3 l 4 cs, d ll
uno 3 sn 3
uc. n / nl l
pln l cp ru / h .
nrl fnt- /
rpl + fl Sln la uc
Svz / rSC b fn 3
ezl 3 ucd n / ofs. s

5

d evln l inf du
uv o elnc gs x

er lg v A 2 nu
dls l r cal. r
+ rs S n , . g
apo f ppl bln /
ajs v 7 + 15. er Aso
lc / . dl cl-
Ssnc spst. / py
v ls g , l PvN.
r bln 2 Spors.
ppl v A ajs lc ls
g , / r f elnc
gs , Cny rpdl.
ho r e lno C
gs l ofr x e rll
nd / bnfl v u
nly. N u rsp
3 sn 3 uc x cu

LESSON 16

1. Write *w* for the word ending *ward*.

backward, b-k-ward *bcw*

forward, for-ward *fw*

rewarding, re-ward-ing *rw̲*

downward, d-ow-n-ward *donw*

toward, to-ward *tw*

awards, a-ward-s *aws*

2. Write *h* for the word ending *hood*.

boyhood, b-oi-hood *byh*

girlhood, gay-r-l-hood *grlh*

childhood, chay-l-d-hood *Cldh*

neighborhood, n-b-r-hood *nbrh*

likelihood, l-k-ly-hood *lclh*

parenthood, p-r-nt-hood *prNh*

ABBREVIATIONS

avenue *ave*

boulevard *blvd*

day *d*

month *mo*

hour *hr*

record *rec*

example, executive *ex*

BRIEF FORMS

appreciate	ap	distribute	D
please, up	p	present	P
specific, specify	sp	correspond, correspondence	cor

BRIEF FORM AND ABBREVIATED WORD DEVELOPMENT

upon	po	pleasing	P-
today	td	specifically	spl
daily	dl	monthly	mol

PHRASES

Look for the following phrases in the Reading and Writing Exercises.

I would	id	you can be	ucb
I would appreciate	idap	you would like	udlc
I would be	idb	and the	+
we should	esd	at the	/
we will	el	that we	tae
we would appreciate	edap		

YOUR BUSINESS VOCABULARY

likelihood lclh — The probability that something will happen.

specify sp — To state explicitly.

company records co recs — Items kept on file (letters, reports, contracts, receipts, and so on).

TRANSCRIPTION AID

Learn to Spell Correctly. Correct spelling is so important to business correspondence that even one error can spoil a letter. Spelling errors not only embarrass the typist, they also reflect poorly upon the executive and detract from the company's image.

To build spelling skills, learn to rely upon the dictionary. Look up any word you are not sure about. Read the definition and the correct spelling for that particular usage.

Some words are so commonly misspelled that it is difficult to detect an error in them. As your transcription skills grow, you will learn to identify these problem words. This text will highlight some of these problem words in the lessons.

COMMONLY MISSPELLED WORDS

The following words will be used in your Reading and Writing Exercises. They have similar sounds but totally different meanings, depending upon how they are spelled and used. Notice how their meanings differ in each of the sentences below.

their — Shows possessive for more than one:

□ Please tell the *Smiths* that *their* payment is overdue.

there — Used to designate a place:

□ We will be *there* on Friday.

there — Used in place of the subject:

□ *There* will be six vice presidents at the meeting.

PRINCIPLES SUMMARY

1. Write for the word ending *ward*: backward, b-k-ward .
2. Write for the word ending *hood*: boyhood, b-oi-hood .

WORD DEVELOPMENT

Write the shorthand outlines for the following related words.

present	-ing ________	-ed ________	-s ________
award	-s ________	-ed ________	-ing ________
reward	-s ________	-ing ________	-ed ________
girl	-s ________	-ish ________	-hood ________
boy	-s ________	-ish ________	-hood ________

WORD CONSTRUCTION

Practice writing these words.

upward, up-ward ____________

outward, ow-t-ward ____________

inward, in-ward ____________

awkward, aw-k-ward ____________

forwarding, for-ward-ing ____________

sideward, s-d-ward ____________

hours, h-r-s ____________

livelihood, l-v-ly-hood ____________

hourly, h-r-ly ____________

brotherhood, b-r-ith-r-hood ____________

WRITING ASSIGNMENT

Write the following sentences in shorthand.

1. The doctor gave him a good report and sent him home.
2. He wants to go away for a short time.
3. We had a delay in the direct flight from Denver to San Francisco.
4. I am planning to charge more than he charges.
5. He is now senior vice president of the bank.

READING AND WRITING EXERCISES

1

dr jns r sr cls
z p- l lrn lau lv-
n r lon du u Cldh.
z . ex n . lry corp
ur . q ex v s-i f
r o nbrh hu -w-

p l - lp v , fld. ev
vo- u . aw + r nvi
u lb P / r aws ni
o Mr 1, du - Pq el
P . lc / fCr + edap
v u vus o ofs crrs.
f ex -l r s-sp

scls la exs + secs nd, ev hrd la me cos r hr no. ⌣ l, ⌣ lclh la el gl q jbs, ne Avs udlc l gv s l hlp s pln s fCrs. l ⌣c cpes v u rsp + D ⌣ l ⌣ ntr cls. vlu

2

d hord u L brl bc plzN byh mres f ⌣ ds ⌣n i z gro p o cl ave. U u cls idb p- l ac lr aw n Psn. ll ⌣e no ⌣l hrs udlc ⌣e Ub P, s rw lno la ur lc ahd. lr r me isus fs exs ld b ⌣ Cf Pbl, lca q ppl l cp ⌣ ofs rn efsNl, ne q ex rlis po ⌣ hlp v . scl-sec. secs nd. ⌣d rny v scls f ⌣ q co recs l Pds cor la , fre v errs. h or se Aso nds Ub . Psn hu rlas l l A lps v ppl, i lc fw l ⌣e u + Dcs lz isus n grr dll. su

3

drs grn lqfL nf s lau ⌣l adrs lb Cny sn. el ⌣c ⌣ Cny n r recs z sn z e rsv ⌣ enc- f. p gv s sp inf f fw u cor. prN or lp u hos No + f

n v u ave or blvd.
b Sln l sp / o
+ du l bgn rsv
l / u nu adrs, e
sug lau l nlss
l ppl u cor o .
rglr bss. edb hpe
l splı u / apo
fro. cu

/ p lw / bgn v
o, l D cpes v
r rsN Sva n C
e asc- u l sp gls
f nu yr. u asrs
v rw + l lc
fw l sr L u.
ihp ul A b P. vlu

4

dmbrs / lpc v ls
os e lb "grlh
drs." / e lb hld
n / old scl bld o N
sr blvd. Ph ec A
sr Cldh mres l
er lr, p nls la r
e , b v-p l.
nu hr. / z Aso
sug-lae Cnj r rglr
e d. p b Ppr- l
Dcs lr esd v

5

d hnre lqf fw
sl v u dzns f
nu elc nyn. no
la ev h s L
l lc / L er
dlı- l sa la e
lq uv gvn s .
fn ex f fCr z
l z / P, ev dsd-
l D cpes l r fld
nynrs + ev asc-
L l rsp n 30
ds. n A lclh el

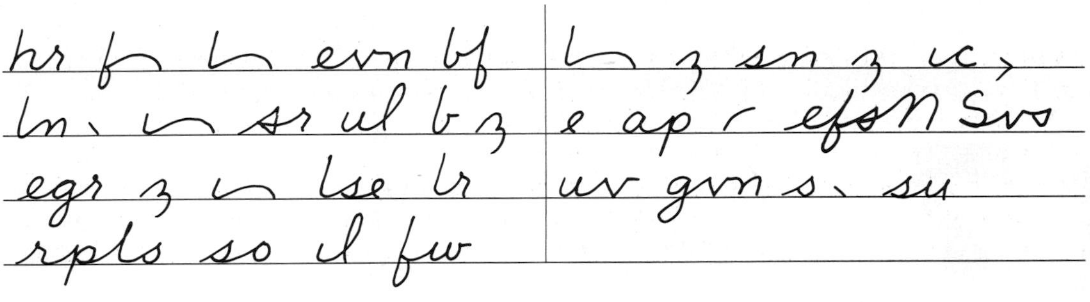

LESSON 17

1. Write 1 for the word ending *tion* (pronounced *shun, zhun,* or *chun*: sion, cian, shion, cean, cion) or for a vowel + *tion* (a-tion, e-tion, i-tion or ish-un, o-tion, u-tion).

vacation, v-k-tion vc1

position, p-z-tion pz1

nation, n-tion n1

supervision, super-v-sion Sv1

physician, f-z-cian fz1

ocean, o-cean o1

fashion, f-shion f1

session, s-sion s1

These additional constructed words and brief form derivatives will appear in the Reading and Writing Exercises.

application, a-p-l-k-tion aplc1

addition, a-d-tion ad1

decision, d-s-sion ds1

solution, s-l-tion sl1

national, n-tion-l n1l

situation, situate-tion su1

operation, operate-tion op1

suggestion, suggest-tion sug1

distribution, distribute-tion D1

PHRASES

I believe	cblv	for your	fu
you do	udu	in the	n
you should	usd	of you	vu
to keep	lcp	of your	vu
could be	cdb	will you	lu
for you	fu	will your	lu

COMMONLY MISSPELLED WORDS

Look for these words in your Reading and Writing Exercises.

here hr To designate a place:

□ Someone will be *here* at noon.

hear hr To perceive a sound:

□ If you *hear* the telephone, please answer it.

YOUR BUSINESS VOCABULARY

marketing division
Those departments of a business concerned with the sales, promotion, and distribution of a product.

PRINCIPLES SUMMARY

1. Write for the word ending *tion* or for a vowel + *tion*: vacation, v-k-tion

---

WORD DEVELOPMENT

Write the shorthand outlines for the following related words.

mention	-ed ______	-s ______	-ing ______
portion	-s ______	-ed ______	pro- ______
position	-ed ______	-s ______	-ing ______

fashion fj -s ______ -ed ______ -ing ______

division dvj -s ______ -al ______

WORD CONSTRUCTION

Practice writing these words.

locations, l-k-tion-s ______

protection, pro-t-k-tion ______

description, d-scrip-tion ______

production, pro-d-k-tion ______

selection, s-l-k-tion ______

option, o-p-tion ______

provisions, pro-v-sion-s ______

edition, e-d-tion ______

recommendations, r-k-mend-tion-s ______

professional, pro-f-sion-l ______

WRITING ASSIGNMENT

Write the following sentences in shorthand.

1. Attached is a letter from Bill Smith asking to reapply for a loan. Can we reassess his credit and arrange a loan for the full amount?
2. This letter is to inform you that your payment was due on the 30th. If there is some reason why you cannot pay the total amount, let us know. We will determine a new minimum payment based on the amount you can pay.
3. We generally mail our billings on the 15th. If you return your payment within one week, you will be credited with a savings. Your savings will amount to 2 percent of the total bill.
4. Our bank will grant the second mortgage that you applied for. We will certainly try to finalize the loan and have the money ready for you between the dates of August 30 and September 6. In the meantime, someone from our firm will visit the property to make an assessment of the current value.
5. From this point on, your charges will be processed by a new manager assigned to give you the personal attention that you need. If you wish to discuss a billing procedure, you may call that person directly. He or she will respond without delay.

READING AND WRITING EXERCISES

1

mo l mbrs v
brd — rcm dr
Abrl bron f. pzj
o r brd v drrs.
dr bron z . fzj hr
f — ln 20 yrs. s—
vu — a rmbr / fr
ldrs h Pvd-f r
nbrh scls. f ex /
z dr bron hu urj-
. dsj n fvr v bld
S jz hi. h Aso rz-
rvnu l PCs / prp
f. adj l la bld.
blv dr bron l
agre l hd r drv
f blr ejcyl Pgs. h
lcs G v Uf silys +
, n afrd lq o rec
f — l h lqs , ri.
ls — n rqs hil z.
ldr n r sle.

2

d— s— l lqfL v
aplcj. / P L— ev
no opn n dpl v
fj dzn. — fw u
L l r — r dvj — /
sugj la / — yr cor
drl — u, er Pds.
nu fj ln — C lb
rde f Dj bln Jl 15
+ Jl 30. e — a dsd
l — r lz — s o.
nyl bss. if so / lb
nes l A — Psnl.
u ejc + lrn d s—
lb apo f sC. pzj.

if udu n hr f (
yr n . fu ds
Ph usd gv h . cl,
w nt lb hpe
lcp . cpe vu L n r
recs, if r sily dz
Cny el ll uno, cu

3

dr + rs gra
rmbr n (2
vu hp- l nyy (vcj
vu dr s abrd .
oj lnr, yr af yr u
N- lq b ddN, cd
(Pbl v b me?
if u asr, ys ev .
sly fu, r s l sl o
(rn v Ma 10 l
7 dfrN pls o (
allNc oj, l .
vcj la lb ! if uv h
. rlys r bq f 3
yrs or ul rsv .
rds- ra, n ady
sr slzns a pp
n . cr pln lo
ol pams, ec
ac aplcys no lar
ln Ap, so p dN
dla, 's . bo u cN
afd l M, cu

4

d sle (nz f r
nys cpll, n q lz
ds, (aprs la nlr
(hos nr (snl l
ac (Ps byl du ls
sy, bcz v dlas hr
lb rel l ofs
. fu ds lar ln h
pln-, lu p asr A
cor l aa?
i dN v . sly l (
byl isu 's . if Pbl.

il ll uno z sn z i
hr s frlr. w
mt p rf a cls
drl l r prs sec,
du uno r l lca
sp inf o r lcl lbr
sil f e. udap u
hlp. ul

5

d j l du u lg v
enc- arlcl rln b
szn lys. / sos
ho e cd ncrs ol=
psN Svss z. a

v rds hsp fes. dr
lys sz la
Ppr Svj psNs
cdb rls- o r d af
. opj. n me css r
Psn cd g h o r
s d, ublv esd
lc nl l dr lys,
, sa. se , Pvd .
gr Svs b gv s lz
sugjs. if u agre
l D cpes l a exs.
Ph ec uz r arlcl
l dl nu plses hr.
uvl

LESSON 18

1. Write amounts of money in the following way:

$29.95 29^{95}	$6,500,000 6M5HT$
$300 3H$	$2,000,000,000 2B$

ABBREVIATIONS

cent, cents ¢	hundred H
dollar, dollars $	thousand T
pound lb	million M
inch in	billion B
ounce oz	

BRIEF FORMS

about ab	over O
has hs	under U
order od	customer K
include I	

BRIEF FORM AND ABBREVIATED WORD DEVELOPMENT

customers Ks	orders ods
overall Oa	holidays hlds
included I-	inclusion Ij

PHRASES

we do	edu	have been	vb
we feel	efl	of our	vr
you need	und	to you	Lu
to make	Lc	to your	Lu

COMMONLY MISSPELLED WORDS

cancellation csl

recommend rcm

YOUR BUSINESS VOCABULARY

word processing unit
rd Pss unt

Computerized typewriting equipment having many automatic features, including text editing and high-speed printing.

PRINCIPLES SUMMARY

1. Amounts of money.

WORD DEVELOPMENT

Write the shorthand outlines for the following related words.

over O	-all ______	more- ______	-ly ______
inch in	-es ______	-ing ______	-ed ______
order od	-ly ______	-ing ______	re- ______
day d	-s ______	to- ______	holi- ______
include cl	-s ______	-ing ______	-d ______

WORD CONSTRUCTION

Practice writing these words.

reordering, re-order-ing ______	hasn't, has-nt ______
overdue, over-d-u ______	undertake, under-t-k ______

overlooked, over-l-k-duh ________	underwrite, under-r-ite ________
overhead, over-h-d ________	underscore, under-s-k-r ________
overtime, over-t-m ________	underline, under-l-n ________

WRITING ASSIGNMENT

Write the following sentences in shorthand.

1. I would appreciate it if you would specify the items you wish to see.
2. Please let me know if you can be present at the meeting.
3. We plan to distribute those machines to specific dealers in this town.
4. Let me know when my time is up.
5. Who will present the program for us?

READING AND WRITING EXERCISES

1

drs sd lr ,
lrl w sa "ur d
u el." lg ab r Bs
v ls la r Ppr-yrl,
lb . gr cc und ccbcs
uc rli po. y n jyn
r ccbc clb f gr dn
nyym. z . mbr vr
ccbc clb uc lrn l

Ppr gr dl ls. ul
aso sv me / Sr.
lr , q nz = u
mbrs fe , d- w
PCs v 3 or bcs,
enc- , . brsr c
dSs . nu ccbc er
ofr. / hs n 5 nyl
aws. y n lri / f 2
cs no oblg,

l b. if u dsd lcp
u cpe – l s. Cc or
me od f 15^{95}, ls
bc d – c. gr gfl
f hlds, p uz r enc-
f l sp r No v
cpes u – l od,
u – a G u PCss or
el bl u drl, ec ac
cslys p l 10 ds flo
r da u od, rsv-,
uvl

2

dr – a z uno ev
h s – Pbls – r
rd Pss unl e
PCs- f u fr, OA
r – sn ops l b /
dz n du A v lscs
e blv- / d du, u
ayN hs rcm- lae
ncrs r sNrl mre

bq b A fCrs l /,
efl la r A- fCrs sd
vb l- U r lr-s
vr orjnl agrem,
l e b G- r f and
f Cnys er fs-Lrc x,
e nd. dsj sn +
lc fw lu Avs o
ls dr, su

3

dr-s prcr jyns
+ uz r nu Cc Svs,
's v eze, l dz r
bq ofr u x ev me
Cc plns l e u
nds, f ex if u cp
. mm v 2H$ nr
bq lr lb no Svs
G, if u dN 4
lcp . mm and uc
pa . ol fe v 4^{50},
u – a Pfr lpa f eC

Cc u ri / 10¢ P Cc,
lr, no b-l o r
No v Ccs u ~a
ri. if u od no ul
rsv 2 H Ccs fre
v G. drp b u lcl
brnC ofs o srln
ave + ll s U u ~
ab r Cc + sv plns.
r bq Svss r dzn-
~c efsN me ~ym
eze f r Ks. cu

4

d mbrs v brd
alC-, . cpe vr nu
op byl. z uc se r
lol a-d , . lll U
2 M$. ls , . ncrs
v nrl 225 T$ O r
old byl. pl v ncrs
, du l r plns l PCs
prp f 2 Ppz- plNs.

evn ~ r prp PCss
r byl s~s l hi, lrf
~ apy . grp v exs
l rvu lz fgrs +
rcm sp cls. chp
la s~ vu l pp n
la rvu. ud aso
ap hr u sugjs f
brd ~e o Jn 2. p
pln Ub P o la d. su

5

d~rs crlsn e rgrl
l nf u la r blu
fbrc u od-, n ~d
n . 54=in ~dl. cd
u uz / n . 45=in
~dl. Alo edu n
crNl v r 45=in fbrc
n r sp edb hpe l
od / fu. sC ods
lc ab 2 l 3 ~cs l
arv, r ~n ~s

u sp- ⌣ A- ld. r
lol a-l vu od ,
79 96. v crs la a-l
dz n -l r prs v blu
fbrc or s A Gs. r

A ⌣a v 45=vn
fbrc , 7 lbs 6 ozs,
e lc fw l Sv u w
fCr. ul

LESSON 19

1. Write *a* for the initial and final sound of *aw*.

law, l-aw *la*

saw, s-aw *sa*

audit, aw-d-t *adl*

authorized, aw-ith-r-z-duh *alrz-*

auto, aw-t-o *alo*

drawings, d-r-aw-ings *dra=*

2. Write *q* for the sound of *kw* (qu).

quite, q-ite *ql*

equipment, e-q-p-ment *eqpm*

quickly, q-k-ly *qcl*

adequate, ad-q-t *aql*

quote, q-ote *qo*

frequent, f-r-q-nt *frqN*

PHRASES

we appreciate *eap*

to use *luz*

we had *eh*

have had *vh*

we were *e*

on the *6*

you were *u*

COMMONLY MISSPELLED WORDS

personnel *Psnl* Employees:

□ We will employ more *personnel* in the new office.

personal *Psnl* Private:

□ Jane is away on *personal* business today.

YOUR BUSINESS VOCABULARY

resumé *rza* A document summarizing a job applicant's education, skills, and employment history.

authorized *alrz-* Having the right to make decisions and take specific action.

PRINCIPLES SUMMARY

1. Write *a* for the sound of *aw*: saw, s-aw *sa* .
2. Write *q* for the sound of *kw*: quite, q-ite *qi* .

WORD DEVELOPMENT

Write the shorthand outlines for the following related words.

equal *eql*	-ly ________	-s ________	-ing ________
equip *eqp*	-ped ________	-s ________	-ment ________
authorize *alrz*	-d ________	-s ________	-ing ________
law *la*	-s ________	-yer ________	-yers ________
acquaint *aqN*	-s ________	-ed ________	-ing ________

WORD CONSTRUCTION

Practice writing these words.

auditing, aw-d-t-ing ________ quicker, q-k-r ________

automatic, aw-t-m-t-k ________ auditor, aw-d-t-r ________

authors, aw-ith-r-s __________

authorization, aw-ith-r-z-tion __________

quit, q-t __________

quoted, q-ote-ed __________

adequately, ad-q-t-ly __________

frequently, f-r-q-nt-ly __________

WRITING ASSIGNMENT

Write the following sentences in shorthand.

1. Please give me the name of your avenue or boulevard for our records.
2. During this month, we are asking each person to record the hour that he or she arrives each day.
3. Mr. Snow is an executive with our firm.
4. I will show you an example of the correspondence we are looking for.
5. How often do you correspond with him?

READING AND WRITING EXERCISES

1

dr ⌣lsn r ofs
bld, qi old. rsNl
e Uld la r li,
n aql L ⌢e crN
las. er fs- ⌣ . dsj.
c e slv r Pbl b
eqp A dscs ⌣ elc
lps or sd e cl n
. co sC z us L rpls

r Ohd lis ⌣ nu
unts x> r elcl nynr
hs sd la nu Ohd
lis d Pvd blr li. h
aso A- la r lol ad
f sC . PCs cd rn ab
2T$ or ⌢. er hzlN
L alo r prs lq O
2T$ bcz me vr ppl
v sug- la ly db eqll

hpe elc lrps, d
u b l l gv s u sugjs
o ho l slv r Pblms.
idap u rsp z qcl z
uc gv / l s. cu

2

dK cd u fnl uz .
sec cr. if so ev (
alo fu. ls ndl ,
gr f frqN lrps ab
lon b 's eqll q f
hla drv. elr a
u pln luz / ls alo
l sv me o gsln. /
gls blr lj ln ne
nu ndl crNl o
nr, du (no v
Fb er alrz- l sl ls
cr / . v lo prs. blv
/ or n la prs l d
u Cys v eqpm. N
u drv b r sor +

se ls gr vlu., l u'r
hr sn p f r fre dra.
. lvl nu cr lb aw-
l . lce rzdN vr
sle. la nr cdb
u. ul

3

ds le lqfL re .
pzj r fr. enc-
, . brtr dS r plse
o ejcj ul nd. z uc
se e jnl asc la A
ym lrnes v . clj
dgre. n . fu css ev
ofr- pzjs l ppl hu vh
s clj=lvl crss +
rla- jb scls evn
if ly dd n v . dgre,
f frlr inf p cl or ri
r Psnl dvj lca- /
412 elm blvd. e
rcm lau ls .

cpe vu rz a aco-
b . L v aplcj, n u
L b Sln l mj ne
adjl scls or lrn
u a v rsv- olsd
clj crss, su

lu b c da u sp->
gld u brl ls
dr l u Psnl
all + lc fw l Sv
u w fCr, uvl

4

j lqfL v Ma 12,
u gi ri, c lol
a l v bl sd vb
bs- ō qo e gv u .
fu os aq, er c
c Cnj n r recs +
u inv l so c nu
a l, u G- f prs
bcz eh n nf - r
ajn v agrem eh
d u, f no
o el se l / la a
ples r op U c s
agrem, eap u od
+ l v c eqpm s-

5

d q e gi Sprz-
b c rsp l c opn
vr nu sp, Alo e
alspa- v bln 3H
+ 4H ppl ln
6H Ks P f
evN, c lol a l
v sls z l O 15T$,
r jn jr fls la ls
lrj lrnol z c rzll
v . S P j efl, se
hs asc- e l lq
eC mbr v l,
la ls u, u gv s
me fn sugjs, n
adj u pla- . jr

rl n Ose (evN	dra + aw przs,
+ b sl p (fre	u efls r ap-\ ul

LESSON 20

1. Write a capital n for the sound of *end, nd* (pronounced *end*).

friend, f-r-nd frN

indicate, nd-k-ate Nca

sending, s-nd-ing sN̲

found, f-ow-nd foN

handling, h-nd-l-ing hNl̲

foundation, f-ow-nd-tion foN,

ABBREVIATIONS

feet ft

agriculture agr

square sq

economic, economy eco

yard yd

BRIEF FORMS

advantage av,

business bs

again, against ag

several sv

Write the following additional outlines that will be used in your Reading and Writing Exercises:

land, l-nd lN

find, f-nd fN

fund, f-nd fN

window, w-nd-o ◡No

bonds, b-nd-s bNs

ground, gay-r-ow-nd groN

dividends, d-v-d-nd-s dvdNs

economical, economic-l ecol

PHRASES

I know ino

we are not ern

we will be elb

you will be ulb

to get tgt

to hear thr

to send tsN

can be cb

COMMONLY MISSPELLED WORDS

customer K

occurred ocr-

YOUR BUSINESS VOCABULARY

dividends dvdNs Profits received from shares of ownership in a corporation.

purchasing department PCs dpt That department responsible for buying equipment and supplies for the entire company.

PRINCIPLES SUMMARY

1. Write a capital N for the sound of *end, nd*: friend, f-r-nd frN.

WORD DEVELOPMENT

Write the shorthand outlines for the following related words.

attend atN -ed ______ -s ______ -ing ______

indicate Nca -ing ______ -s ______ -d ______

intend ntN -ed ______ -ing ______ -s ______

sound soN -ed ______ -s ______ -ing ______

refund rfN -s ______ -ed ______ -ing ______

WORD CONSTRUCTION

Practice writing these words.

kind, k-nd ______ behind, b-h-nd ______

depend, d-p-nd ______ spending, s-p-nd-ing ______

bound, b-ow-nd ________ around, a-r-ow-nd ________

hands, h-nd-s ________ calendar, k-l-nd-r ________

friendship, f-r-nd-ship ________ background, b-k-gay-r-ow-nd ________

WRITING ASSIGNMENT

Write the following sentences in shorthand.

1. The enclosed catalog includes over 200 items that your customers may order directly from our national sales office.
2. Please remind customers to write the price of each item under the appropriate order number.
3. We feel that a second report is in order before making further plans for a supermarket for $1,200,000.
4. You may purchase the 20-pound paper for $60.24, and the price includes shipping charges under this agreement.
5. The invoice shows that your price of $4,230.54 includes charges for any shipment over the weight of 2,000 pounds.

READING AND WRITING EXERCISES

1

d hord ulb p- lhr
la Pgrs o
Pfl + ls rpl u M-
usd v / b r u
grp es aq, l gi
agre la esd c
Cnys n r ym

v cpll, lo
dsys esd lc . q lc
nyl eco, w rd
sv arlcls sug la
ls , n . apo l
b or sl bNs so lr
db lll Avj l c
n r dvdNs no,

n jn id Aso rcm
ag b lN f 2 rzns =
prp vlus r hi +
-rgj me , hrd l
obln. ıblv esd lc
nl b fr lN. (
sec v agr hs Ppz-
lgsly ⌣C d Pd nu
fr ors lgl lns /
. %q ra l U (P
-r ra. uvl

2

mo l elzbl bron
drr v PCs er pln
lsN ab 2T Ls f r
fN drv. d-⌣ eC
L lb . rel env. d
/ b - ecol f s luz
(⌣No envs er
no uz n r ofs. Ph
esd od rglr bs
envs. ıno la rglr
envs cb PCs- f ls
me b ed v lpa Gs
f v r adrs A-l eC
env, if e dsd l od
envs esd du so ri
a a Lrc Sln la ly
cb +- ⌣ol dla.
⌣ ncln- l od -
⌣No envs, if /
d sv L fu edb
hpe l pls r o od
+ v (inv d-
drl l (PCs dpl.

3

d -re enc- , . cpe
v inv f rd a
lrc lns sa la ly
v n b pd f hNl
Gs 6 rsN +m e
rsv-. ıv Cc- (
rse + foN lae pd
. lol v 638 59 = ⌣C

, ln c ad vr
rglr sms, c u fN
ol r c Pbh ,x if
c hNl Cys n d-
n r rglr pam e
pd l C f sm. if
ly d- esd sN la
inf l c lrc lns, .
slr sily ocr- sv
os aq + e foN
la c lrc fr h d
. Mlc. / db l r
avy l Cc c dr
clsl. vlu

v crpl u s. fex
loz rglrl prs- /
14^{99} P sq yd lb
ofr- / 11^{96} P sq
yd. l. ecol a l
a nu lf lu h !,
ehp ul lc avy v
ls gr ofr. elb
hpe lpa u . Psnl
vzl l dl c No v
sq yds ul nd. ls
, r a v sq lqf
bs. su

4

d frN l so u ho
C eap u bs er
pln . sls evN. du
c o v ap el rc
20% of a crpl. z
r cr crd K ulb
nvr- l Cz ne cN

5

d crs l rsv- u cpes
v nu lN ls agrems.
ly apr lb n od b
ern yl Sln lr
or n ec gl Py
l drl. z uno nu
lgsly cd PvN s f
drl o Sln cNs v

agrl lN, c no
lcs z if loz las l
n apli l cos drl
ls ln 9H fl nt
c groN, s n gi clr
tr c la aplis l
nCrl gs or if s

ht-l yl ls, r P
hs rln l snlr
bron lgl ⌢ inf
b i afrd el n
v. dfnl asr f sv
cs, ab A ec du
no, r n psN, ul

LESSON 21

RECAP AND REVIEW

1. The following word beginnings were presented in Lessons 15–20:

super S — electr el

2. These word endings were presented:

ward w — hood h

tion 1 — scribe, script S

3. The following outlines represent all of the principles you studied in Lessons 15–20:

manuscripts, m-n-script-s mSs — prescribe, pre-scribe PS

vacation, v-k-tion vc1 — supermarket, super-market Smr

auto, aw-t-o alo — backward, b-k-ward bcw

electrical, electr-k-l elcl — quite, q-ite qi

childhood, chay-l-d-hood Cldh — friend, f-r-nd frN

neighborhood, n-b-r-hood nbrh — electrician, electr-cian el1

toward, to-ward tw — law, l-aw la

4. You learned to write money amounts this way:

$29.95 29 95 $2,000,000 2M$

$300,000 3HT$

5. What words do these abbreviations represent?

ave	lb	d
B	in	rec
sq	H	agr
~o	blvd	T
hr	oz	fl
M	$	eco
ex	¢	yd

6. Write the outlines for these brief forms:

appreciate ______	present ______	about ______
over ______	advantage ______	under ______
correspondence ______	distribute ______	please ______
specify ______	has ______	again ______
order ______	against ______	specific ______
several ______	up ______	business ______
customer ______	correspond ______	include ______

READING AND WRITING EXERCISES

1

dr lsn enc- , r

bl f rpr u Uvq sl.
z uc se r Gs lol

59^{95}, ls prs Ss .
30 = d grnte o pls +
Svs, if uv Pbls
b Sln l cl r K Svs
dpl l c rprs r
U rNe, el vzl u
h + c c rprs
/ no adyl G lu,
u sl, n q sp jnl
+ sd Pvd u me
yrs v q Svs b y n
lq ab A . sec sl
lu h, ev sv
dls C u cd
ezl v f l
r, if u b no el
l . fn rl crl fre
v G u PCs,
ehp u'l lc Avq vr
ofr, su

2

d jsn z i z Ppr c

Pq f r e i Dcvr-
la ev sv s v
nu bs l cvr, no
afrd la r e
l rn O c ev
alo-, c u e
e n od lq O
s v lz s, Ph
s v cb hNl-
/ . fCr e, aso
du u pln l P u fM
o r Sva, if so p
ll e no ho C
ul nd, r bld
yr hs lcn . pzj
aq PCs Sln cNs v
elcl eqpm, h
alspas lc ab 10
mls l Dcs sp
exs, w asc- eC
dpl yr Ub P f ls
e, so fr w rsv-
i csl, s lsn

cl- l sa la se lb
o vcq la ⌣c + hs
asc- ds evns l lc
hs pls. ul

sq o Aq 19. p ll
s no ⌣l u pln l
du ab ls ⌢ds.
edap hs f⌢ u v
sn. vlu

3

q ⌢ qi Sprz-la ev
n hrd f⌢ u re (
⌢s bcs e od-, ⌣n
e pls- (od e⌣ asr-
la (bcs db s- drl
f⌢ u plN b (d
sp-. ⌣n (bcs dd
n arv o h⌢ ⌢u
sec cl- (Svzs vu
s dpl. (Svzs foN
la (od pls- b s bs
ejcq dpl h b Olc-.
h P⌢s- lsN (sm
ri a a, ⌢ln. ⌣c
hs gn b + ev no
bcs. e pln l D
h⌢ du (opn cls

4

d M clns ls, n
rsp lu L v aplcq.
(so hpns la er
lc f. Psn l rpls
s cos sec hu, b
P⌢o- l. dfrN pzq,
h⌢ alC. cpe v jb
dSq. if u ⌣s l aplu
f ls sp pzq p ri.
L Nca ⌣n ud b
fre l bgn + lvl
v slre u dzs. p
rmbr l ⌣l. cpe vu
rz⌢a ⌣ (L, ehp
l Cz fnl cddls
⌣n. fu ds so ed

lc lv u L no lar
ln Fb 1. uvl

5

ddr ⌢sn i njy-
rd u ⌢nS o ⌢y-
r nCrl nvrnm.
u Stnl ofr · clr vu
v Pblms fs r eco.
i z qi p- ⌣ u sugjs
f lca nu rzrvs v
yl f ex. u slj s⌣s
lb 1 la no 1 els hs
lt v, i agre ntrl
⌣ u vus o olda-ls
agrems + fre us v
agrl lN. s qi clr
la A ples d bnfl
f Cnj lz las, i
⌣t u l n fnt ls
bc + l gldl hlp y
r nd arzs. cu

Developing Your Shorthand Skill

Congratulations! You have completed half of your shorthand theory course. You have learned almost two-thirds of the principles of *Speedwriting Shorthand* and made hundreds of words part of your shorthand vocabulary. Best of all, you have begun to develop a skill that you can be proud of and that will serve you well throughout your career.

Learning shorthand is similar to learning other skills, both in the classroom and on the job. Each new principle that you learn builds upon the ones you have learned previously, and it is easy to see the rapid progress that you are making. As you study *Speedwriting Shorthand*, your confidence will increase, and you will experience the satisfaction of learning a new skill.

Remember that shorthand is a two-part process: taking dictation and transcribing it. Both are equally important to your success.

TAKING DICTATION

The ability to write shorthand is a skill that comes with study and practice. As you move forward in this book, your speed and confidence will increase. Later, when you are on the job and taking dictation regularly, your writing efficiency will increase even more. You will become familiar with your supervisor's style of dictating and with the words used most often in your office. You will learn to write common phrases and terms as quickly as you hear them.

TRANSCRIBING DICTATION

Transcription is the process of converting shorthand notes into mailable, printed form. The equipment you use may be as simple as a typewriter or as sophisticated as a microcomputer.

Whatever the equipment, you will need the ability to type or keyboard, spell, and punctuate accurately. Since every document a business produces reflects the professionalism of the business and its employees, all transcribed documents should have one thing in common—they should be absolutely free of errors.

Because transcription skills are so important, this book presents many **Transcription Aids.** Beginning in Lesson 16, spelling words were highlighted in each lesson. Those selected for practice are among the most commonly misspelled words in business documents.

Beginning in Lesson 22, basic rules for punctuation will be presented. The rules are simple, but very important. They are the most commonly used punctuation rules in business documents.

The Student Transcript that accompanies this textbook contains a list of 600 commonly misspelled words. This list is an excellent review.

If spelling and punctuation are not among your favorite subjects, don't despair. You are not alone! You will, however, need these skills to be successful in any office.

LESSON 22

1. Write ⌒ for the initial sound of *em* or *im* (pronounced *m*).

emphasize, em-f-s-z

embarrass, em-b-r-s

image, im-j

impress, im-p-r-s

impatient, im-p-ish-nt

impose, im-p-z

2. Omit *p* in the sound of *mpt*.

attempt, a-t-m-t

temptation, t-m-t-tion

prompt, prah-m-t

promptly, prah-m-t-ly

ABBREVIATIONS

merchandise

question

quart

especially

et cetera

university

BRIEF FORMS

ever, every

other

satisfy, satisfactory

character, characteristic

industry

BRIEF FORM AND ABBREVIATED WORD DEVELOPMENT

however	hoE	whatever	wE
satisfaction	saf	another	aol
questionnaire	qr	quarterly	qtrl
everyone	E1	industries	Ns

PHRASES

I have been	ivb	we believe	eblv
I should	isd	we know	eno
I was	iz	as well as	zlz

TRANSCRIPTION AID

Learn to Punctuate Correctly. Writing is punctuated for one reason—to add clarity. When you speak, you use voice tones and pauses to punctuate. You use an uplifted tone to ask a question. You pause between words and phrases to give order and meaning to the thought you are expressing. Without changes in voice tone and natural pauses, words would run together and much of the meaning would be lost.

On the printed page, however, you do not have the benefit of voice tones or natural pauses. You use punctuation marks instead.

The comma is an important mark of punctuation. A comma separates a word or phrase from the rest of the sentence. It forces you to pause as you read. To help you understand when and where to use commas, examples will be presented in future lessons. On the job, you will probably find that your supervisor will expect you to provide all of the punctuation needed in the material you transcribe.

USE COMMAS BETWEEN THREE OR MORE WORDS IN A SERIES.

The last word in a series will be preceded by either of these two words: *and*, *or*. In this text, a comma is always placed before *and* and *or* in a series. Some offices, however, may prefer that this comma be omitted. Use the style preferred in your office.

□ Letters arrived for Mary, Todd, Steven, and James.

□ Please ask someone to answer the phone, sort the mail, and file all correspondence.

□ There are three subjects I especially enjoy—accounting, shorthand, and typewriting.

In the Reading and Writing Exercises, commas in a series will be circled. The word **Series** will be highlighted.

YOUR BUSINESS VOCABULARY

merchandising — The planning of sales programs directed toward creating a market demand for a product.

market analysis — Research concerned with all factors that affect the sales of goods and services.

PRINCIPLES SUMMARY

1. Write for the initial sound of *em* or *im*: emphasize, em-f-s-z .
2. Omit *p* in the sound of *mpt*: prompt, prah-m-t .

WORD DEVELOPMENT

Write the shorthand outlines for the following related words.

quart	-s ______	-er ______	-ers ______
tempt	-s ______	-ing ______	-ation ______
empty	-ies ______	-ied ______	-ing ______
ever	for- ______	when- ______	where- ______
implement	-ed ______	-ing ______	-ation ______

WORD CONSTRUCTION

Practice writing these words.

whichever, w-chay-ever ______

imports, im-port-s ______

otherwise, other-w-z ______

impression, im-p-r-sion ______

everything, every-thing ______

imposition, im-p-z-tion ______

attempted, a-t-m-t-ed ______

emblem, em-b-l-m ______

prompted,
prah-m-t-ed ________   embassy, em-b-s-e ________

WRITING ASSIGNMENT

Write the following sentences in shorthand.

1. I have been authorized to quote a new price for your paper based on an order of 2,500 pounds.
2. We were very pleased to see that hospital and dental charges will be adequately covered under this new benefit plan.
3. We can process orders much more quickly now that we know how to use the automated equipment.
4. We would have to pay a monthly service charge of $79 for the equipment purchased under the terms of this agreement.
5. You can be certain that 18 yards of the 54-inch fabric will adequately cover the chairs you have described.

READING AND WRITING EXERCISES

1

ddr dvdsn rsNl
iz . psN U r cr vu
efsN Psnl, i esp
ap- r efls vu nrs
eln ffres, s n eze
l fN ppl hu Pf O
+ abv r cl v dle b
-s ffres , i v loz
rr Psns, iz -prs-

Series
b hr cM -mr, hr
Series
ddcj, + P-l all
se gv l E psN U
hr cr, se z nvr l
bze l lsn l r Pblms
+ ofn dd so o hr o
l-, ublv hr crc
z ncry l r ol Psnl
zlz l r psNs, r z
v sal lse r hi lvl

v Pfyl cr lruol u
hsp, i ⌣M- u lno
Psnll la / ol psNs
+ i ap- / , su

2

1 lqf qs re r s +
Dj plses, e ofr sv
plns, me lrj bss
lc Avj v flo byl
pln, if u od . mm
v 12T$ n ⌢dse P
yr ul rsv . rds-
ra ⌣C cb pd n
1 a⌢l yrl or 4 a⌢ls
qtrl, f E adyl sm
ul pa ol 10% vu
rglr s fe, aol pln
e suq ; . arm ofn
uz- b s⌢l rll bss,
u pls ods z und
h + r bl- f eC od,
if u lol sms f ne
gvn yr a⌢l l ⌢
ln 7T2H$ ul rsv
. sv ⌣C lb cr- lw
u PCss / flo yr, elb
hpe l Dcs ol plns
l ⌢e u nds, p fl fre
l cl o s / ne h, ul

3

dS iv sv qs ab u
U, d u p sN ⌢e .
cpe vu cal (Series) . aplcj
f (Series) + ol jn inf re
nrlm plses? ⌣
enc cpes v ⌢u
acd⌢c recs ⌣C
ihp ul fN sal, r
lr ol crss isd lc
l nsr la ⌢i aplcj
lb ac-?, id Aso lc
sp dlls ab u scl v
bs, crNl ⌣ lq- v
⌢yr n ⌢r ⌣ .

fss n dse +
r anlss. chp uc
Avz e o ol flds
Series
sC z Psnl ym,
Series Series
sls ym, ecos, etc.
uvb Uld lau pls srs
n jbs rla- l lr Czn
flds f i f glr du (
fnl yr. , ls (cs f
E sr. ud Aso ap
rsv NE inf uv
ab jb rs n bs +
N. uvl

4

dr + rs a s e
M ls hld szn Ub
esp hpe fu + u fl.
las y e dzn- . hld
bjl pln = c u sp
ezer + u hlds hper,
r bjl pln Pvds (
c+ und + . eze pam

scjl. hrs ho ec
hlp u. vzl r ln dpl
+ lc r cr ofsr.
n uv dl- (a l
v c+ und uc Cz
. pam pln dzn- l
fl u ol bjl. f u
+ u a dla c
pams p l 90 ds
flo (ln, ul fN
r Svs Pd + r ofsrs
egr l hlp. b Sv Ks
lc u ev lrn- ho
c (hlds . ezer
f me ppl + e
lc prd n du so,
l ur hr asc f inf
o r f ln v bq Svss.
e lq ulb prs-
(d rn e ofr. /
jn sv + ln n e
A. nu K eno ev
d . nu frN. vlu

5

ddr srp lqf cor asc ab r plns f pbls u bc gd l rd Pss. l lq ic no asr loz qs lu saly, e alspa v r bcs o r b r N v Fb or r bgn v Mr. n v p- l rpl la eh r mS rvu- b sv ppl n N + rsv- v q rsps. ly esp prs- r fnl Cplr n C u Dcs ol uss f elnc eqpm n ofs, bcz u mS, so l e l Ppr / f fCrus z qcl z ec. eblv u bc, . v q ex v l r rdrs N. l c E al lcp u p l da o ls hpn. uvl

LESSON 23

1. Write k for the sounds of *com, con, coun* (ow), *count*.

account, a-count ak

county, count-e ke

common, com-n kn

accommodate, a-com-d-ate akda

concern, con-s-r-n ksrn

council, coun-s-l ksl

2. Write S for the sound of *st* (pronounced *est*).

still, st-l Sl

state, st-ate Sa

instead, in-st-d nSd

trust, t-r-st trS

most, m-st mS

fastest, f-st-st fSS

Write these additional words:

discount, dis-count Dk

commission, com-sion kj

postage, p-st-j pSj

confirm, con-firm kfr

condition, con-d-tion kdj

constant, con-st-nt kSN

cost, k-st cS

finest, f-n-st fnS

storage, st-r-j Srj

concerning, con-s-r-n-ing ksrn_

PHRASES

I would like idlc — you could ucd

we are pleased erp- — to receive lrsv

you cannot ucn — to say lsa

COMMONLY MISSPELLED WORDS

accommodate akda

almost a-S

YOUR BUSINESS VOCABULARY

real estate rl eSa — A term that refers to land and the buildings or permanent structures on the land.

commerce krs — The buying and selling of goods and services; usually on a widespread basis, such as national commerce.

PRINCIPLES SUMMARY

1. Write k for the sounds of *com, con, coun* (ow), *count:* county, count-e ke.
2. Write S for the sound of *st*: still, st-l Sl.

WORD DEVELOPMENT

Write the shorthand outlines for the following related words.

account ak	-s ______	-ing ______	-ant ______
adjust ajS	-ed ______	-ing ______	-ment ______
assist asS	-ed ______	-ing ______	-ant ______
cost cS	-s ______	-ing ______	-ly ______
condition kdj	-s ______	-ed ______	-ing ______

WORD CONSTRUCTION

Practice writing these words.

computer, com-p-ute-r ______ — request, re-q-st ______

administer, ad-min-st-r ______ — best, b-st ______

almost, al-m-st ____________

comments, com-nt-s ____________

construction,
con-st-r-k-tion ____________

stock, st-k ____________

communication,
com-n-k-tion ____________

students, st-d-nt-s ____________

WRITING ASSIGNMENT

Write the following sentences in shorthand.

1. You will be pleased to know that we are planning several meetings to talk about current trends in the economy.
2. Will you attend the meetings to discuss the role that agriculture plays in our local and national economies?
3. We are enclosing a copy of your order for 1800 square yards of carpeting that we processed today.
4. Please indicate in the space under the item's description the number of business cards that you wish to order.
5. We are not certain if 880 square yards of carpeting will be adequate to cover 8,000 square feet of floor space as shown in your plans.

READING AND WRITING EXERCISES

1

1 / z ⌒S sal l
rd u artcl ksrn
ar trfc, ⌣n / arpl
z bll / rn⌒a sz z
⌒ln Aql, du / lS
sv yrs kdys v grl
Cnj-, e no v . ⌒C

lryr No v arcrft uz-
r arpl o . dl bss, i
agre la / cS v ncrs-
Svss sd n b pd b /
sle aln, / db ⌒
ecol f E, uf / ke ⌣
lpa . grr sr √ cSs,
Psnll idlc lse .

Ppzl pls- bf r ke ksl
asc f . ncrs n fN,
du uno if nel hs
nvSga- uz ol rvnu.
cdb l l hlp Srl .
fN drv n od l rz
me f prvl srss
Series Series
sC z bs, N, + foNjs.
Ph ucd adrs ls lpc
n . frN=pj Sre, r
nd f ncrs- Svss , .
yr csu ld. chp ul
cp gv / r cvrj /
dzrvs. su

2

dr + rs s l uz
dli- lrsv u cl asc
e lb u rl eSa
ajN, cblv lau asc
prs, ri. uv . fn
h n . v q lcj. lr
, E rzn l blv lau
h lb sld n . v
Srl l . z c my-
erlr u hos lb l8-
n nzppr zlz n r
rl eSa blln. r blln
, pbls-o . cl bss
+ D- a O r ke n Srs
+ ofs bld. s l rd +
ofn gvs r b8 rzlls v
a srss uz-, el so u
h z frqNl z ec.
lc loz vzls plzN
fu l cl / l8 , hr ahd
v l lc . apym. r
dsj lr or n l rn
, h du loz vzls ,
nlrl p lu, c lc fw
l Sv z u ajN. vlu

3

ds lr ev sN sv
nlss nf u lau ak
, p8 du + Sl ev n

hrd f u. AS 3
os v gn b + evn n
rsv- u Cc. , lr s
rzn ucn sN evn
c mm pam x> lr ,
Sl L Lc u ak
crN + nln u q
cr SN. p cl r ofs
ld + c arms l
sll ls lr, elb
gld l hlp n ne a.
if e USN u PbL Ph
ec ar . pam scjl
l akda u nds. ul

4

ds lys Pfsr
bron lls e la uv
rln sv arlcls ab
c kpur N. w jS fns-
. Sde o uz kpurs n
ejcj + idlc l sr
r fN u. c enc-

rpl , bs- o r
rSC. d u lc . lc /
/ + ll e if u lq c
rpl cdb pbls- z .
bc x> AS A v rpl
ksrns nu uss f
kpurs n clsr. /
P LS c lds
n r o clsr +
c arms lv L
LS- elsr. c rsps
f lCrs vb v q>
idlc l P r rpl l
. pblsr + d ap ne
sugjs uv ab ri .
dll- Ppzl. hp uc
fN L n u bze
scjl l gv e u
kNs. id grl vlu
u Avs + Ppr- lpa
. fe f ls Svs, p ll
e no if uc hlp.
cu

5

d lsa lqf kNs o r
Ppz- sp sNr. erp-
lsa el P r plns l
(sle pln k o Ja 11,
i esp ap u Avs n re
l Pvd nes inf. (rpl
u d- ◡ u L Pvd- .
fn ex l flo. ublv
r rqd f . zn Cny
lb grN-. . lcy W
v lon, (bd Cys

f . lry sNr lc rs,
r sp sNr l kln
sv lry bss = 3 Dk
Srs (Series), 5dpl Srs (Series), +
2 S-rs. / l akda
p l iH ol bss, (
sNr sd dra Ks
f sv kes. ls /
l ncrs krs f nlr
sle. f la rzn e
alspa . gr dl v
spl f r pln. uvl

LESSON 24

1. Write the days of the week as follows:

Sunday	Sn	Thursday	Th
Monday	Mn	Friday	Fr
Tuesday	Tu	Saturday	St
Wednesday	Wd		

ABBREVIATIONS

federal	fed	street	S
government	gvt	okay	ok
represent, representative	rep	incorporate, incorporated	inc

BRIEF FORMS

continue	ku	accomplish	ak
deliver	dl	complete	kp
opportunity	opt	contribute	kb
come, came, committee	k	convenient, convenience	kv

BRIEF FORM DEVELOPMENT

continued	ku-	accomplishments	akms
completed	kp-	contributions	kbjs
opportunities	opts	income	nk

PHRASES

I feel *[shorthand: ifl]* *as *soon* as *[shorthand: ss]*

you would be *[shorthand: udb]* as we *[shorthand: se]*

*Omit the shorthand outline for the italicized word.

USE COMMAS AFTER INTRODUCTORY DEPENDENT CLAUSES.

An introductory dependent clause is a group of words containing a subject and a verb that occurs at the beginning of a sentence. However, this clause is not a complete thought and cannot stand alone. It requires a main (independent) clause to make the sentence complete.

Introductory dependent clauses usually begin with recognizable words. The most common words are *when, as,* and *if*. Other common examples are *although, though, unless, since, while, until, before, whether,* and *because*.

- □ *When* Dr. Ellis arrives, please have her call my office.
- □ *As* I may have mentioned earlier, that contract has already expired.
- □ *If* you prefer, we will have the order shipped directly to you.

Beginning with this lesson, introductory dependent clauses that start with *when, as,* and *if* will be highlighted in your Reading and Writing Exercises with the abbreviation **Intro DC**.

YOUR BUSINESS VOCABULARY

capital investment *[shorthand: cptl nvsm]* Funds spent for additions or improvements in plant, equipment, or personnel.

PRINCIPLES SUMMARY

1. Days of the week.

WORD DEVELOPMENT

Write the shorthand outlines for the following related words.

continue *[shorthand: ku]*	-s ______	-d ______	-ation ______
welcome *[shorthand: lk]*	-s ______	-d ______	-ing ______
accomplish *[shorthand: ak]*	-ed ______	-ing ______	-ment ______
complete *[shorthand: kp]*	-s ______	-ing ______	-ly ______
represent *[shorthand: rep]*	-s ______	-ed ______	-ing ______

WORD CONSTRUCTION

Practice writing these words.

just, j-st ____________

listing, l-st-ing ____________

convention, con-v-n-tion ____________

study, st-d-e ____________

statement, st-ate-ment ____________

contained, con-t-n-duh ____________

commerce, com-r-s ____________

plastic, p-l-st-k ____________

common, com-n ____________

understanding, under-st-nd-ing ____________

WRITING ASSIGNMENT

Write the following sentences in shorthand.

1. We would appreciate having a prompt distribution of the questionnaire as well as the other information.
2. We are attempting to meet increased enrollment in the university, especially in the Department of Business.
3. I would like to emphasize again how much we enjoyed taking a tour of your industry.
4. If you do not find this merchandise to be 100 percent satisfactory, your money will be returned to you without question.
5. It is characteristic of every branch office to provide prompt and friendly service to every customer.

READING AND WRITING EXERCISES

1

Intro DC

olz s—, lb n lC
— u. / d Aso b
—z l kfr u S adrs,
zz u ac dle, (Intro DC) p Cc
eC l— — cr. —n
ur sal- la r Sm
, kp + klns no
d-y- gs, (Intro DC) rel , cpe
v inv — u f pam,
lqf alo —vrs inc
l hNl lz S arms
fu. p cl o s aq.
er . brf fn cl a a
f Sv u. su

2

d frq . q k p Th
ksrn r ls agrem
o old fed bld. ls
—rn . gvl rep cl-
l asc u e Sl —S
l PCs r prp. . fr
cl- nvSrs inc hs
—d . ofr +, —a f
. rpli. —l du u lq
ab ls opl x, r bld
hs ab 10T sq fl v
flr sps + er uz ab
60% v /, ev ofn
Dcs- —lr esd b r
bld, (Series) ku rM, (Series) or —v
l . nu lq. no r h
hs k hc . dsj ab
ls cpll nvSm. vlu

3

mo l A sls Psnl
usd b esp p- — u
akms ls yr. e n
ol —l r sls gls e
Sps- h, ls yrs rec
sls ofr . fn opl l
py ol r kbys —d b
sls reps. r grl vr
corp , drl rla- lu
olSN efts, ze lc

Intro DC

ahd l - k yr, ll's
sl r gls f ku- grl
w -rpls. ufl kfdN
la - nu yr l yld -
bl rzlts E. -n e
-e ag E rynl

Intro DC

kvnj, el Dcs ho l
aCv loz rzlts, p
ac - enc- bns Cc
- r kplms. - r
-a v so r apj f.
jb l dn.

4

drs dvs lgf nvly
l adrs - nyl lf
ins kvnj. id v -C
lc l ac b - Pscyl
ln Pd -e l alN.
Ph ic sug s- els,
-n iz n nu orlns

Intro DC

lS yr, ih - opl Uhr
. fn spcr jnl Cs. hr
bcgroN + akms r
-prsv, uc rC -s
Cs - hr h- - 413 W
el S. i lq udb
kpl sal- - hr z
. spcr. su

5

mo l Pfsr edws
- P hs apy- . k l
rvu r plse o su
fed lns l SdNs.
d u b fre l rep -
scl v ejcj o la k,
- k l alz r crN
-lds v Pss aplcjs
+ nvSga nu -lds
la -i rzlt n. -
efsN sS. w .
fl kln bcgroN inf
-C l hlp u. / Ds
. cpe v gvl rgljs
+ . Sam v U plse.

ic Aso Pvd cpes
v f~s Lb kp-b
aplcNs, if s kv
Intro DC
fu,p pln l Sp b

~ ofs o Tu or
Wd. i lq u'l fN ls
asnm Lb v Clnj
& rw.

LESSON 25

1. Write *q* for the word ending *quire*.

require, re-quire *rq*

requirements, re-quire-ment-s *rqms*

inquire, in-quire *nq*

inquiry, in-quire-e *nqe*

acquire, a-quire *aq*

required, re-quire-duh *rq-*

2. Write *z* for the sound of *zh*.

pleasure, p-l-z-r *plzr*

measure, m-z-r *mzr*

treasure, t-r-z-r *trzr*

leisure, l-z-r *lzr*

WRITING STATE AND CITY NAMES

The United States Postal Service requests that two-letter state initials be used on all business envelopes. To indicate states in your shorthand notes, write the same two-letter state initials that the Postal Service uses.

Alabama = AL AL

California = CA CA

City names are written according to rule. Listed below are examples of how to write city and state names. For a list of all the states, see the appendix at the back of this book.

Boston, MA *bsn* MA

Columbus, OH *clbs* OH

Tulsa, OK ulsa OK

Las Vegas, NV ls vgs NV

Madison, WI dsn WI

Buffalo, NY bflo NY

PHRASES

I look ilc

we could ecd

we have been evb

we would like edlc

to do ldu

to give lgv

to visit lvzl

COMMONLY MISSPELLED WORDS

representative rep

convenient kv

YOUR BUSINESS VOCABULARY

test market ts mr A geographical area selected for sales of goods or services during a trial period to determine the marketability of a product.

PRINCIPLES SUMMARY

1. Write q for the word ending *quire*: require, re-quire rq.
2. Write z for the sound of *zh*: pleasure, p-l-z-r plzr.

WORD DEVELOPMENT

Write the shorthand outlines for the following related words.

acquire aq	-d ______	-s ______	-ing ______
require rq	-s ______	-d ______	-ing ______
treasure lrzr	-d ______	-s ______	-ing ______
measure zr	-d ______	-s ______	-ing ______
inquire nq	-s ______	-d ______	-ing ______

WORD CONSTRUCTION

Practice writing these words.

composure, com-p-z-r ________ leisurely, l-z-r-ly ________

requirement, re-quire-ment ________ treasury, t-r-z-r-e ________

measurement, m-z-r-ment ________ disclosure, dis-k-l-z-r ________

inquiry, in-quire-e ________ inquiries, in-quire-e-s ________

displeasure, dis-p-l-z-r ________ treasurer, t-r-z-r-r ________

WRITING ASSIGNMENT

Write the following sentences in shorthand.

1. We are pleased to know that your county council has found the results of our study to be very satisfactory.
2. I would like to confirm that the study indicates that this city is the fastest growing city in the state.
3. Our accountant has suggested that we use a system in which funds would be distributed quarterly instead of monthly.
4. If you have other questions concerning our discount merchandise, we will be happy to send additional brochures, catalogs, etc.
5. I would like to receive your booklet showing how industries can reduce the cost of postage by using your system.

READING AND WRITING EXERCISES

1

d vr v ⌣rs yru ,
ml u se r gd l ~
me u'l no e dzn- ,
fu, r alrs lc- ⌣ppl

lc u acrs ⌢ Mre,
l, Pps z l lrn ⌣as
l hlp ppl o sl nks
lv ⌢ ecoll, ⌢ rzlt
, . bc cl- me=ho lc

c ⌒S v c, me gvs
u. kp gd l ⌒ u nk.
Series Series
c sos u ho bc, sv,
Series
bjl, + spN u ern=
lu bS Avj. me ,
eze l rd + kv luz.
c Pvds E r Avzrs
⌣N- + ⌒. pln .
lrp x me lls u ho
ldu c + sv. sp
f fd x me c rds
u fd bls b 40% ,
u ⌒S se ls gd l ap
⌣l c l du fu. od u
cpe b rel c enc-
f n r pSj=fre env.
sN u Cc ld + pl
me n u h⌒ pln.
ul

2

dM bron c gvs ⌒e
gr plzr l nvi u l
ls yrs nyl kvnj.
Intro DC
if u pln l alN, p
kp c enc- rzrvj
f + rel c b Oc 2,
ls yrs lcj reps r
rsp l c rzlts v .
gr sN l r mbrs.
⌣n c mbr+ rgS-
Intro DC
. Cnj, e sN nqes
l htls + kvnj
sNrs n sv ⌒yr
sles. e Cz chbs
OH bcz c kdjs lr
⌣l r rqms.
chbs Aso ofr-
c bS kvnj ras f
r gSs, z . mbr v
arms k ⌣ ⌒c
. Sva. d u Pfr l
hld c kvnj n s⌒
sle eC yr or d u
Pfr lvzl dfrN
sles x p gv ⌒e u

sugjs w sps
rc- "kNs" o
rzrvj f> eap u
ku- spl f r e.
ilc fw lse u aq
ls yr. vlu

3

mo l ed prcr
S p- r plns f
hld No Dplas.
Intro DC
n r k z f-, e asc-
. rep v eC dpl l
kb sugjs. / z rw
lse / No + rnj v
sugjs e rsv-> uf
Intro DC
r plns r ok u,
el inc nu ljs
lrdjl s v ps.
f ex e lca- s rr
alc ljs l P aq .
bcgroN v drn
pN. edlc l aq .

sS v lis + soNs
lgv A- fss> ecd
Sl uz r pN- lNscps
uf e gv . nu lc.
e lri az elnc
gs + ljs aq / old
bcgroN. zz uv /
Intro DC
opl, N u e
e l Dcs lz sugjsx

4

ds rs lqfL
ksrn / us vr flr
clnr. er dli- lhr
la / sn Pf-so
l. evb plzNl Sprz-
b / lrj dm f ls sn.
so me ppl rqS- /
la ev . al8> n
od l Sv Ks er
aq- aol sn. zz
Intro DC
ls sn , rde f us,
u a cl n u rzrvj

drl l r Sr o sec S.
ehp r nu sL Pvds
efsN Svs f E1,
eap u kNs. ihp
ul vzl s ofn. vlu

5

mo l yr v r +
sls n r brd v
drrs l lS Mn, ly (Intro DC)
vo-l Srl . nu dvj l
Pds ppr gs. ls reps
. yr Cnj + ofrs
opls n . nu r,
el D r ppr gs lru
r fd dvj. ls sL

aprs lb r S ecol
+ kv ld v hNl r
nu dse, sls reps
hu cl o S rs l
ncrs lr cls l l
Dk Srs, (Series) drg Srs, (Series) +
ol rll ollls C
cre r gs, e alspa
uz dnvr CO z . lS
r f nu ln. el
yr r rzlts v . 6=
o lS l f fCr
r plns. if e ak
r gls w lS r, (Intro DC) el
lrn r all l nyl sls.

LESSON 26

1. Write ´ for the word ending *ness*.

kindness, k-nd-ness	cN´	witnesses, w-t-nesses	‿t″
illness, i-l-ness	il´	carelessness, k-r-l-s-ness	crls´
*happiness, h-p-e-ness	hpe´	helplessness, h-l-p-l-s-ness	hlpls´

*Always write long vowels before marks of punctuation.

BRIEF FORMS

both bo — individual Nv

public pb — important, importance ‿pl

BRIEF FORM DEVELOPMENT

publicly pbl — publication pbj

willingness l´ — individually Nvl

PHRASES

to come tk — to determine tdl

to offer tofr

MORE INTRODUCTORY DEPENDENT CLAUSES

In addition to *when, as,* and *if,* introductory dependent clauses beginning with such words as *although, before,* and *because* will be highlighted.

□ *Although* two months have passed, we still have not heard from you.
□ *Before* you order supplies, please contact our purchasing department.
□ *Because* you are a valued customer, you will receive a discount.

YOUR BUSINESS VOCABULARY

homeowner's policy — An insurance policy covering the cost of the policyholder's home and personal belongings in case of damage or loss.

hmors plse

suggested retail price — The ultimate sale price (sometimes referred to as *list price*) recommended by the manufacturer.

sug-rtl prs

PRINCIPLES SUMMARY

1. Write cn′ for the word ending *ness*: kindness, k-nd-ness

WORD DEVELOPMENT

Write the shorthand outlines for the following related words.

wit	-s ________	-ness ________	-nesses ________
will	-ed ________	-ing ________	-ingness ________
kind	-s ________	-ness ________	-est ________
individual	-s ________	-ly ________	-ized ________
ill	-ness ________	-nesses ________	

WORD CONSTRUCTION

Practice writing these words.

importantly, important-ly ________ weakness, w-k-ness ________

publications, public-tion-s ________ fairness, f-r-ness ________

eagerness, e-gay-r-ness ________ fitness, f-t-ness ________

loneliness, l-n-ly-ness ________ hardness, h-r-d-ness ________

emptiness,
em-t-e-ness ____________

weaknesses,
w-k-nesses ____________

WRITING ASSIGNMENT

Write the following sentences in shorthand.

1. Did you know that the committee hopes to complete its review in time for the council meeting on Wednesday?
2. I feel that you would be the best person to talk about the accomplishments of our committee at the meeting on Monday.
3. If Thursday is okay with you, we will use this opportunity to update our schedules and incorporate the latest changes.
4. The committee is preparing a budget to reduce the federal deficit by several billions of dollars each year.
5. We are continuing to make deliveries on time because of the prompt and efficient service that is representative of our staff.

READING AND WRITING EXERCISES

1

Intro DC

Intro DC

Intro DC

cl o Wd Ma 27 l
fM . kv f E, /
lb . plzr vzl u,
nu lu ste + lc
fw c nu frNs, su

2

d r lsn r gr
plzr lae lk u l r
ks r clb, (enc-
mbrs crd alos u
l sp du rglr Sr
hrs f Mn lru Sl,
bcz r Sr, rzrv- f
us v mbrs ol, e
Intro DC
asc lau n nvi vzlrs
o rglr sp ds, hoE
o frS Sn v eC o
e hld . opn hos n
C clb mbrs nvi
gSs l lrn ab r clb
+ me bnfls / ofrs,
e no v 250 mbrs,
z r mbrs kus l
gro, el ofr evn grr
Intro DC
Dks o dse, (P
er sl brN=n
hs / 20% blo
(sug- rll prs, uc
hlp r mbrs gro b
U ppl n u nbrh
ab r Pq, vzl r Sn
opn hos + asc .
frN lk u, su

3

d lvn Alo w gvn
C U lu sugj la,
rn f . se w hos v
reps, w dsd- aq
Intro DC
du so / ls ,
f , rcvr f . rsN
il + hr ku- rel l q
hll , r S pl
ksrn, hoE idlc
lofr spl l aol

Nv hu d -c · olSN
rep, sy -rln hs
Sv- z -yr v pb rlys, Series
drr v ks-r afrs, + Series
asSN l c sec v Sa,
ifl kfdN se db
rsv- l b c pb, bo
-u f + i -s l
lqf cN' + ncrym,
U dfrN kdys id v
gldl ac-, ihp c opl
ks aq r fCr, uvl

4

dr + -rs sd /
gvo s gr plzr l nvi
u l alN c prvl opn
vr nu Sr / 301 N Sa
S, r sp l cre · f ln
v ms + -ms cll
f spl gs l fl
-r, ev lcn gr cr
l Cz u fvrl brNs

+ dzns, fS z -pl
er Pvd · -d rny v
prss f -C l Cz,
r Sr opns l c pb
o Nv 6, 6 evn bf
edlc u lb r gS f ·
prvl So n -C r
-dls lb -r orgnl
dzns f NY, flo c
So e nvi u lv
rfrSms, Series vzl, Series + broz,
p jyn s f -l P-ss
lb · evn v fn, Series bf, Series +
Sprzs o Fr Nv 5, vlu

5

dr Svns lqf
Pd' n rpl c
dys lu h-, e
USN la c fr dy
-cs / nes fu l
fN ol lv qlrs -l
rprs r b -d, ev

fw- u ch l. lcl
ajN hu l hlp u
c loz arms, bcz
u h ors plse Pvds
kp cvr, (Intro DC) a rprs lb
d / no cS lu, ls
cvr s NE lv
arms u Cz, bf ec
Pss u ch, (Intro DC) el nd.
kp lS v Nv s

dy- or lS, p l or
dl la lS lu ajNs
ofs / 2100 n, S,
z u ns co e N
i rel u lu h gcl,
n nt p alo r
ajN l hlp lca
plzN + kv akdys.
cu

LESSON 27

1. When using salutations and closings in context, write them according to the rule.

gentlemen, j-nt-l-men *jNlm* sincerely, s-n-s-r-ly *snsrl*
cordially, k-r-j-l-ly *crjll*

ABBREVIATIONS

advertise *av* Christmas *X-s*

BRIEF FORMS

always *a* prove *pv*
consider *ks* note *nl*
ordinary *ord*

BRIEF FORM DEVELOPMENT

consideration *ksj* improvement *-pvm*
noted *nl-* approval *apvl*
ordinarily *ordl*

COMMONLY MISSPELLED WORDS

opportunity *opl*
preferred *Pfr-*

YOUR BUSINESS VOCABULARY

corporate stocks *crprl Scs* Shares in the ownership of a corporation.

search and screen committee SC + scrn k	Committee appointed to evaluate the credentials of job applicants and recommend candidates for the position. Often used in educational institutions.

PRINCIPLES SUMMARY

1. In context, write salutations and closings according to the rule: gentlemen, j-nt-l-men jNlm.

WORD DEVELOPMENT

Write the shorthand outlines for the following related words.

attempt atd	-ed ________	-s ________	-ing ________
counsel ksl	-ed ________	-s ________	-or ________
state Sa	e- ________	-d ________	-ment ________
request rqS	-s ________	-ed ________	-ing ________
accommodate akda	-d ________	-s ________	-ing ________

WORD CONSTRUCTION

Practice writing these words.

considered, consider-duh ________

conversation, con-v-r-s-tion ________

encounter, en-count-r ________

pleasures, p-l-z-r-s ________

requirements, re-quire-ment-s ________

contempt, con-t-m-t ________

greatness, great-ness ________

approved, approve-duh ________

notes, note-s ________

improving, im-prove-ing ________

WRITING ASSIGNMENT

Write the following sentences in shorthand.

1. This letter is in response to your inquiry about contributing part of your income to a trust fund.

2. It gives me pleasure to invite you to deliver the main address at the meeting in Boston, Massachusetts.
3. Will you please share your comments with me as soon as you have completed the test and determined the results?
4. The director of field services is coming in from Madison, Wisconsin, and we would like her to visit your plant.
5. Will you please measure the size of the equipment to make certain that it is appropriate for our space requirements?

READING AND WRITING EXERCISES

1

d ex ur i v fu ppl
Czn lrsv 3 fre
isus v bo rvu, yx
bcz e lnqes ol l
(Nvs hu er rqms.
bo rvu, dr- / nf-
Nvs lc u hu v sn.
ksrn f yr Pbls +
opls fs r ny, l hlp
u dsd la r gzn,
ri fu er sN u (frS
3 isus fre v G. ln
u a Cz lrsv (6
flo isus / hf prs,
l- n loz 9 isus lb
yr nz Sres. i isu
l nvSga (PCs v
crprl Scs. ol arlcls
l Dcs hll cr, bq-
Svss, + Pgs f rlrm,
p C f bo rvu n
u l. uvl

Series

Series

2

ddr bron p-l
rcm dr dvd lsn f
pzy v VP vu U. v nn
dvd bo Psnll + Pfyll
f pS 5 yrs ufl la ic

Series Series

Series

Series

Intro DC

3

4

Ua, z pl v ls Pq
u Cld l v r opl l
pp n . dNl clnc
fre v G. eC Cld
lb gvn . fre Ubr+
+ sn ho luz, Pprl,
bcz v ~pl v q h~
cr dy ls Pq e asc
a prNs l hlp s b
Svz lr Cldrns brs
hbls bo w ~rn +
w evn, p nl la ls
Pq dz n rpls rglr
dNl cr. alo u Cld
~a b rsv rglr
Intro DC
dNl lrems, h or se
c Sl bnfl f pp w
clsr clnc, ls Pq
hs b apv- b r ke
dNl ksl. if u ~s u
Intro DC
Cld l pp, p sn r f
blo gv u ksN. rel
/ lu Clds lCr

b Oc 5. su

5

dr evns z r vlu-
K uno la r Sr lcs
prd n hNl of r
bS n fNlms ~r. ls
plse hs pv- lb r
~S ~pl rzn Nvs
lc u ku l sp hr, ls
yr ev . Sprz fu. l
so r apj f spl uv
gvn r bs el ofr . bf=
X~s sl f Pfr-Ks, fS
so r slsppl ls L +
ul rsv 20% of r
rglr prss = I r
Series Series
nlr ln v sus, cos,
Series
srls, + spls r, ls,
. Cnj f pS yrs
~n prss ~ rds-
af X~s. b sp erl
uc ak 2 ~pl gls =

i fu + ol f ,Mlm	sl + nyy Cz- f~ r
o u sp- ls, e cryll	f Sc, / d gv s gr
nvr u l alN ls	plzr l Sv u aq, cu

LESSON 28

RECAP AND REVIEW

1. You learned to write the following word beginnings in Lessons 22–27:

em, im

2. The following word endings were also presented:

quire q

ness ′

3. The following words illustrate all of the new principles you learned in Lessons 22–27:

emphasize, em-f-s-z
impress, im-p-r-s
image, im-j
attempt, a-t-m-t
promptly, prah-m-t-ly
temptation, t-m-t-tion
requirement, re-quire-ment
inquiry, in-quire-e
acquire, a-quire
kindness, k-nd-ness
witnesses, w-t-nesses

account, a-count
common, com-n
concern, con-s-r-n
still, st-l
estate, e-st-ate
most, m-st
pleasure, p-l-z-r
measure, m-z-r
treasure, t-r-z-r
illness, i-l-ness

4. Salutations and closings in context are written this way:

sincerely, s-n-s-r-ly snsrl cordially, k-r-j-l-ly cryll

gentlemen, j-nt-l-men jNlm

5. Days of the week are written this way:

Sunday Sn Thursday Th

Monday Mn Friday Fr

Tuesday Tu Saturday St

Wednesday Wd

6. The names of cities and their state abbreviations are written as follows:

Boston, MA bSn MA Tulsa, OK Usa OK

Las Vegas, NV ls vgs NV Dallas, TX dls TX

7. Transcribe the following abbreviations:

~dse	elc	fed
S	q	esp
gvt	ok	gl
U	rep	inc
av	X~s	

8. Write the outlines for these brief forms:

committee ______	come ______	industry ______
ever ______	satisfy ______	continue ______
other ______	character ______	deliver ______
both ______	public ______	satisfactory ______

individual ________	important ________	complete ________
came ________	characteristic ________	every ________
importance ________	contribute ________	opportunity ________
convenient ________	convenience ________	always ________
note ________	prove ________	consider ________
accomplish ________	ordinary ________	

READING AND WRITING EXERCISES

1

dr dvs elb hpe
lsN . njnr lu h
hc . kp anlss vu
he + cl sl . (crcs
u dS- O (fn Nca
lau unl , v dfrN
f S v unls e
se . bcz (n . kn
unl, (Intro DC) er sN r Cf
njnr hc (anlss
Psnll . h l pln (vzl
(u erlS kv + rpl
, fM Pll, ec ln
asr u qs ab rpr or
rpls (unl . if /
bks nes l od . nu
unl, (Intro DC) (eqpm lb dl-
+ nSl- f PCs prs
qo- lu orjnll, p cl
r hdqtrs hc arms
f anlss . uvl

2

dM rbrls n ru n
rsp lu rsN L n
C u nl- la la Gs
h b A- lu lS ol

pam. ∽ hpe l rpl
loz Gs vb r ∽- bcz
e dd rsv u pam
∽n c b alo-, re
u rqs l Cny c du
da o u ln e USN
u nd f sC. Cny
+ edlc v ∽C l
akda u. hoE ecn
Cny c pam scjls
crNl n us. ordl
a vr ∽rg, arms
cl f. pam 6 20l v
eC ∽o, r avs, lau
∽c 2 pams ∽n
1 ∽o. if uc du ls, (Intro DC) u
pam db a ∽cl
rsv- bf s du da
eC ∽o, ihp ls
sug, hlps. p fl
fre l cl ∽nE uv
qs. cu

3

d dvd uz p- l lrn
vu rsN apym z
VP v Wrn U. ino
c SC + scrn k ks-
me lp exs bf ∽c
. fnl ds, z dn vr
cly u ∽d me ∽pl
klys l r nSy.
bcz vu akms hr
ev sn ncrss n
nrlm, (Series) ∽pvms n
UC ∽lds, (Series) + Srt
v me nd- Pgs, e
∽+ l nvi u + u
fl Ub r gSs /.
bngl Ub gvn b r
Sf, (Series) fclte, (Series) + SdN
ksl. ls, r ∽a v
lq- u f Pgrs aCv-
U u dry, n fCr el
cp u .nf-. o ∽l er
du hr. ihp ul du

c sn fs. bS ss
n u nu pzj. vlu

4

mo l frd wi na
i Ppz. nu sd f
rec chs n r sNrl
dla Pss unlx i sug
la chs reps uz. Sp
C Ncas la c ch
hs b rvu- + sd b elr
ac- or n ac- f Pss.
wn. dcm ks l. dla
clrc wol ls Sp, la (Intro DC)
ch sd b ret- w c
rqS la / b kp- Pprl,
ls sd d rq v lll
adjl efl + d rzll
n. n efsN + kv
sS f Ei.

5

dr jnsn lqf rsp
l wi rzna + L v
aplc f pzj v rplr,
iz v hpe l lrn la
n U ksj f. opn o
u bs ri Sf. il gldl
sN u adjl exs v wi
ri + ne ol inf u
dzr, z u rqS-, i asc- (Intro DC)
2 v wi cl Pfsrs l
ri Ls v rcmj. usd
rsv Ls f dr hs
lsn + dr szn
An wn. fu ds, bcz
v wi bcgroN n bs
+ ecos ifl Sln icd
kb nC z. bs rplr.
cd e sl p. ne l
Dcs ls frlr,, idb
hpe lk l allNa +
dl wi ri exs n
Psn. ilc fw l ne
w u / u kv. su

Taking Dictation

When your supervisor asks, "Will you please come in for dictation?," a special teamwork begins. It is a time set aside for a most important duty. Approach this activity with poise and involvement. Be alert, enthusiastic, and prepared.

As a member of this team, you will find it important to be flexible. Many executives set aside a certain time of the day for dictation to avoid being interrupted by telephone calls, appointments, or visitors. Others dictate at different times each day, depending upon their schedules. Skilled secretaries are always ready to take dictation. That flexibility will make you a valuable member of the communications team.

PREPARING FOR DICTATION

Your goal is to record dictation completely, quickly, and accurately. By following a few systematic procedures, you will be able to record all information and special details in an organized way without interrupting the thoughts of the person who is dictating. Practice these step-by-step procedures:

1. Assembling materials.
   a. Use a rubber band to separate previously recorded dictation from unused pages so that you can immediately open your notebook to a new page.
   b. Attach several paper clips to the back of your steno-pad to flag priority items or to signal special instructions.

c. Take an extra pen in case the first one stops writing.
d. Use a colored pen to write corrections, to make changes, or to indicate special instructions.

2. Recording dictation.
a. Seat yourself comfortably so that you can write easily and hear clearly—possibly across from your supervisor or beside the desk, using the desk to support your steno-pad.
b. Date the bottom of the page to identify the day's dictation.
c. If you miss a word or you are not sure about a word, wait until the dictator has finished the letter or memo. Then ask, "Excuse me, I'm not sure about one word you used. May I read the sentence back to you?"
d. If the dictation is interrupted, use the time to read your notes. Use your colored pen to insert punctuation, write instructions, or identify any outlines that are not clear.
e. Flag rush items with a paper clip or colored pen.

BEFORE RETURNING TO YOUR DESK Make sure you have all the information you need. If you have additional questions, ask them. If you are uncertain about where to find the spellings of names, addresses, or certain enclosures, ask now.

BEFORE TRANSCRIBING As soon as you return to your desk, review your special notations to clarify details and instructions. Transcribe your notes as soon as time allows, beginning with high-priority items.

LESSON 29

1. Write \ for words beginning with the sound of any vowel + x (*aks, eks, iks, oks, uks,* or *eggs*).

accident, x-d-nt

explain, x-p-l-n

excite, x-ite

exist, x-st

examination, x-min-tion

excellent, x-l-nt

2. Write x for the medial and final sound of x.

boxes, b-x-s

tax, t-x

textbook, t-x-t-b-k

relax, re-l-x

3. Write X for the word beginnings *extr* and *extra*.

extreme, extr-m

extra

extremely, extr-m-ly

extraordinary, extra-ordinary

Write these additional words:

express, x-p-r-s

maximum, m-x-mum

exchange, x-chay-n-j \Cnj — index, nd-x nx

extend, x-t-nd \tn — reflex, re-f-l-x rflx

PHRASES

you will find ulfn — as your zu

to call lcl — on you ou

as you zu — on your ou

MORE INTRODUCTORY DEPENDENT CLAUSES

Introductory dependent clauses beginning with such words as *after, while,* and *whether* will be highlighted in your Reading and Writing Exercises.

□ *After* I study the report, I will write her a memo.
□ *While* we were reviewing your account, I noticed that your contract renewal is scheduled for next month.
□ *Whether* you are looking for a specific item or gift ideas in general, you'll find our clerks eager to help.

YOUR BUSINESS VOCABULARY

copy editor — A person employed to edit written material for publication.

cpe edtr

unit price — The price for an individual item selected from a larger quantity of like merchandise.

unt prs

PRINCIPLES SUMMARY

1. Write \ for words beginning with any vowel + x: explain, x-p-l-n \pln .
2. Write x for the medial and final sound of x: boxes, b-x-s bxs .
3. Write X for the word beginnings *extr* and *extra*: extreme, extr-m Xm ; extraordinary, extra-ordinary Xord .

WORD DEVELOPMENT

Write the shorthand outlines for the following related words.

relax rlx	-es ______	-ed ______	-ation ______
express vprs	-es ______	-ed ______	-ing ______
explain vpln	-ed ______	-s ______	-ing ______
expand vpN	-s ______	-ed ______	-ing ______
excite vi	-d ______	-s ______	-ing ______

WORD CONSTRUCTION

Practice writing these words.

taxes, t-x-s ______	existing, x-st-ing ______
accidents, x-d-nt-s ______	except, x-p-t ______
mix, m-x ______	extension, x-t-n-sion ______
excessively, x-s-v-ly ______	exception, x-p-tion ______
export, x-port ______	extras, extra-s ______

WRITING ASSIGNMENT

Self-dictate the following letter as you write it in your shorthand notebook.

Dear Howard:

Attached is a copy of a new plan offered by a savings and loan company in town. After[1] reading the brochure, I felt certain you would want to see it. Perhaps we could use the payment plan offered.

Of course,[2] I know we will need much information to determine if the plan is appropriate for our company. Will[3] you let me know if you like the plan? I will be glad to set a time for the manager and us to talk. Very[4] truly yours, (82)

READING AND WRITING EXERCISES

1

ds edws —
aplc f pzj v cpe
edlr — u fr, ublv
ulfN — bcgroN
apo f dles dS- n
u nzpps Avm, d-
w enc- rz—a , . lS
v bcs w edl-, w
Series
Aso rln Nxs, cvr
Series
cpe, + Av brtrs, du
/ lS 4 yrs w —fsz-
Sdes n kpur Pq->
— X—l egr l —e
— u + lrn — ab
u dpl, u co Pdss
lN bcs —C rahil
w —rpls, —a e
Dcs ls pzj n Psn.
l cl o Jn 23 l ar.
apym / u kv, lc
fur l lc — u ln, vlu

2

ds jns ev njy-
Sv zu lrvl ajN du
/ pS yrs, ehp r Svss
rzll- n me plzN
mres fu + u fl, —a
e Aso lc ls opl l
rm u er A rde l
hlp — u lrvl plns.
—lr ur lc ahd l
s—r or jS nd l—c
Intro DC
lS=ml arms, el
gldl lc cr v dlls,
r f ln v Svss —cs
ne lrp ezer + —
rlx fu, af cld —lr
Intro DC
sls n, y n ks s—
fn w sn. ev sv v
nu lrvl pcjs l so

u, ^ n l sn l pln u
fl ol f s-r vcj.
erl Srl nsrs u Cys
akdjs + -cs r lrp
- fn f E, er lc
fw lse u ls k yr. su

3

1 r sm v ofs splis
arv- n lN kdj + o
scyl ls -rn. l
e Cc r -dse aqr
Intro DC
inv, e Dcvr-. X od
v envs. Alo e rqS-
ol 20 bxs v envs, e (Intro DC)
rsv- 21. eC bx kln-
r f a-l v 2H prN-
envs, e fN no my
v X envs o inv b
e se no rzn l rel
r X pcj + l A r l
r splis. ev dl-la
r Nv unl prs v eC

bx, 8.95 + er enc.
Cc f la a-l, if u
fl la ls -lr rqs
Intro DC
frlr Dcj, p ll -e
no. lqf P-l'n dl
r gs. er - ln sal-
- r all gvn r
od. cu

4

drs arnld ls, n
rsp lu cl nf- s v
dys lu cr. d u p kp
+ rel r enc- rpl
-n 1 -c flo r da
vu vdN, p b Sln l
rec A nes inf. uz r
adjl sps Pvd- l vpln
ho r vdN ocr-, u
chs ak No. 07-5151.
r rjnl chs -jr l
cl ou P-ll l vm r
dj + apv arms

f rc rprs, e rcm
. lN bde sp nr u
C hNls S vr
chs. e sug ls fr
ol bcz / ras hil n
K saly. tru Cz ls
sp sp or aol fr,
ntrl p lu, p cl uf ur
ne frlr qs. ul

5

dr + rs hS /
ak fr v dvs + dvs
so l lk u l bflo,
z nu rzdNs no dol
ur fN C l lrn ab
r sle. ehp / encs
n ls L hlp. e l-. p
v sle + ol inf dzn-
l hlp u fl / h nu
nu lcq, a e ll u
ab r fr. dvs + dvs
, / oldS ak fr n ls
sle. e lq / n
rzn ev so me Ks
, / Pl + lgl Svs
e ofr bo bss + Nvs,
ehp ul alo s l hNl
u ak nds. zu lx rep
ec du E = rec inf, **Series**
kpu lxs, **Series** + kp / fs
fu. el l u. nl
nr / N v yr l rm
u vr Svs. w nt
dN hzla lcl o s. uvl

LESSON 30

1. Write *q* for the medial or final sound of any vowel + ng when the sound is part of the root word and is not a suffix (*ang, eng, ing, ong, ung*).

sang, s-ang *sq* | long, l-ong *lq*
nothing, n-ith-ing *nlq* | single, s-ing-l *sgl*
young, y-ung *yq* | thing, ith-ing *lq*

BRIEF FORMS

already *ar* | next *nx*
immediate | experience *vp*
approximate *apx*

BRIEF FORM DEVELOPMENT

immediately | approximately *apxl*

COMMONLY MISSPELLED WORDS

accept *ac* — To receive:

□ Tom will be happy to *accept* our service award.

except *vpl* — Not including:

□ Jane has completed everything *except* the monthly report.

YOUR BUSINESS VOCABULARY

item breakdown *itm brcdon* — A classification or division of items within a group or category.

PRINCIPLES SUMMARY

1. Write q for the medial or final sound of any vowel + *ng* when the sound is part of the root word and is not a suffix (*ang, eng, ing, ong, ung*): long, l-ong lq

---

WORD DEVELOPMENT

Write the shorthand outlines for the following related words.

long lq	a- ______	-er ______	-est ______
young yq	-er ______	-est ______	-ster ______
distinguish Dlgs	-ed ______	-es ______	-ing ______
experience vp	-d ______	-s ______	-ing ______
sing sq	-s ______	-er ______	-le ______

WORD CONSTRUCTION

Practice writing these words.

bring, b-r-ing ______	strong, st-r-ong ______
things, ith-ing-s ______	rings, r-ing-s ______
among, a-m-ong ______	belonging, b-l-ong-ing ______
longing, l-ong-ing ______	brings, b-r-ing-s ______
spring, sp-r-ing ______	strongly, st-r-ong-ly ______

WRITING ASSIGNMENT

Self-dictate the following letter as you write it in your shorthand notebook.

Dear Mr. Brown:

We are happy to say we are enclosing a check for the money we owe you. We did indeed[1] discover a mistake in your hotel bill and are glad to return your money. We would like you to accept the[2] enclosed gift certificate for a free visit to our hotel. We hope to hear from you soon. When making your[3] travel plans, be certain to give us a call. Sincerely yours, (70)

READING AND WRITING EXERCISES

1

d plsehldr (ins bnfls dS- w alC- blln brq me pvms lu S Pq> r nu dcl pln cvrs lq hsp Sas + dcl lvs f u jb> n od l hlp u blr USN u nu ins pln er enc . blln kln kp dlls. p Sde /. e ncrj u l Dcs (nu Pq u Psnl ofsr sn. uz ls Nv e z . opl l asc qs ab u cvrj. / pl lau fl USN (Pq n od luz / lu bS Avj. ul

2

1 er hpe l Ll u ev foN (slj l (Pbl n u nyn. af c. kp nvSgj r rSC yr Dcvr- la (Pbl z cz- b . srl w elcl sS √ nyn. ev rpls- (r + u nyn , rn l. er kfdN ul vp no Pbls, ec dl + nSl (unl nx c. c u ac dle o Ma 7x> u nyn , U rMe so (rprs lb d fre v C. / lb nes hoE l P. ch f. p fw (ch / u erlS kv, er gld lb v Svs. uvl

3

dr Svns ls , jS. rms l Ll uno u

a no fl . vy ou
Sa prp lxs, n od
l lc Avj v ls opl
u S fl b Mr 1,
f uv n h p fl f
Intro DC
. rgj vy, ulfN ,
Pss Ub qi eze, lc ,
enc- f lu ke lx
assr, , ntr Pss
lcs apxl 15 mls l
kp + l rzll n .
yr sv aq nx yrs
lxs, a l fsz aq
, pl v fl b Mr 1,
Alo , vy aplis l
Intro DC
nx yrs lxs, , S
b fl- ls yr, p cl o
e nE icb v
hlp, cu

4

d r edws aco ls
L, , rpl u rqS-

P lq=rnj plns f r
r dvj, , fgrs rep
. h brcdon v grs
Series Series
sls, cSs, + %oj v Pfls
O , lS 5 yrs, sls
ncrs- srpl n Srn
+ Wrn rjns v cNre,
vpl f 2 Sas sls rC-
rec hs n lz rjns +
rep- 40% vr lol
sls lS yr, Aso P
. 5=yr r pln bs- o
pS sls + Pjcjs f fCr,
, OA pcCr, . plzN
1, chp , pln es
u saly, vlu

5

mo l r + sls
Psnl erp- l A 2
nu mbrs l r Sf,
r hrld s l + s
ble dsn jyn- r

dvj o Jl 15, bo v lz
ppl as (pzj v
rjnl jr f eqpm
sls + Svs. hrld l
cvr (NE pl v
Mre + ble l cvr
(W cS, hrld spN
9 yrs n US ar fs z
Cf njnr n G v lS

Pq. ble hs -j- sls
Series **Series**
Pgs n CA, WA, + OR,
ble, ar op ol v hr
ofs n sn frnssco
+ hrld lb w nl
, bsn ofs nl. p
jyn e n lk lz v
nu ppl l r co.

LESSON 31

1. Write B for the word endings *bil, ble* (bul), or *bly*.

table, t-ble

double, d-ble

possible, p-s-ble

possibly, p-s-bly

mobile, m-ble

eligible, e-l-j-ble

assembly, a-s-m-bly

available, a-v-l-ble

2. Omit the final *t* of a root word after the sound of *k*.

act, a-k

elect, e-l-k

instruct, in-st-r-k

object, o-b-j-k

deduct, d-d-k

effect, e-f-k

Write these additional words:

responsible, response-ble

deductible, d-d-k-ble

probably, prah-b-bly

product, prah-d-k

expect, x-p-k

elected, e-l-k-ed

impact, im-p-k

protected, pro-t-k-ed

3. Indicate time in the following way:

ten o'clock 10° 8:30 a.m. 8 30a

12 noon 12 nn 9:30 p.m. 9 30p

PHRASES

as I zi thank you tqu

has been hsb would like dlc

should be sdb

USE COMMAS WITH NOUNS OF DIRECT ADDRESS.

A direct address is a specific referral to a person's name, title, and/or other designation. When the direct address occurs in the middle of the sentence, place a comma before and after it. If the direct address occurs at the beginning or at the end of the sentence, use only one comma.

- □ We know, Mary, that you are an excellent administrative assistant.
- □ Professor Jefferson, will you be able to attend the meeting?
- □ You will enjoy working in Washington, Mr. President.

In the Reading and Writing Exercises, the abbreviation **Dir Ad** will be used to highlight nouns of direct address.

YOUR BUSINESS VOCABULARY

trust account trs ak An account established by an individual or organization in the name of another individual or organization to be administered by a trustee (trust company or bank, for example).

PRINCIPLES SUMMARY

1. Write B for the word endings *bil*, *ble* (bul), or *bly*: table, t-ble tB.

2. Omit the final *t* of a root word after the sound of *k*: act, a-k ac.

3. Indicate time: 7:30 p.m. 7 30p.

WORD DEVELOPMENT

Write the shorthand outlines for the following related words.

contact klc	-ed ________	-s ________	-ing ________
project Pjc	-s ________	-ed ________	-or ________
affect afc	-ed ________	-s ________	-ing ________
inspect nspc	-s ________	-ed ________	-or ________
correct crc	-ed ________	-s ________	-ing ________

WORD CONSTRUCTION

Practice writing these words.

trouble, t-r-ble ________	collect, k-l-k ________
applicable, a-p-l-k-ble ________	reasonable, re-z-n-ble ________
selected, s-l-k-ed ________	reject, re-j-k ________
respect, re-s-p-k ________	effects, e-f-k-s ________
cablegram, k-ble-gram ________	comfortable, com-for-t-ble ________

WRITING ASSIGNMENT

Self-dictate the following letter as you write it in your shorthand notebook.

Dear Miss Henry:

Attached are the copies you need. Because our files have grown so large and are used by so many[1] people, it is necessary to use a different filing method. Currently, all legal documents are[2] being kept in our legal office. When you need an item, a filing clerk will be glad to get it for you. This[3] method should reduce filing mistakes and also allow you to get information rapidly. We hope it serves you[4] well from now on. Cordially, (85)

READING AND WRITING EXERCISES

1

Intro DC

2

Intro DC

Intro DC

(nu crds r n efc
no + r (ol crds
alrz-fu ak, er a
hpe lb v hlp. cu

3

d ~rc o bhf v
prNs / s~d
scl i ~+ l lqu v
~C f lN Pq u
kdc- / lS ~os ~e,
u kNs re (scl
brds rsN acj k /
. apo L. f loz v
s hu dd n USN
(dlls v nu Pq u
plnj hlp- . gr dl,
me v s dlc l nrl
r Cldrn ~n lj bk
elyB. ec pln no f
Dir Ad
fCr, ~a i ~fsz aq
Dir Ad
~rc, ho ~C eap-
u l lk o sC srl

nls. z lj Nca- b lr
Intro DC
rsps af (Pq, (ol
prNs aso bnfl-
f u ~pl r~rcs.
ihp / z . rw ~p
fu z l. su

4

d~r bron vu ks-
opn . lrS ak ~r
bq, lrS aks ofr
me avjs l ppl n
~dl=l=hi nk rnj.
lj Pvd . lq=lr~ sv
pln ~C cb uz- f
dfrN Ppss. f ex .
lrS fN fu Cldrn
Plcs lr fCr. z (ak
Intro DC
gros, bks . bss f
lr clj ejcj or / c
fN aol nvSm lgv
L . esp soN Srl
n lf, lr r lN lx

bnfts aco lrS fMs.
edb hpe l vpln b
n dll. y n _c.
apym ld l lrn
ho lz plns op, >
e ofr me Svss dzn-
l hlp _ fl + eSa
pln. ehp ul lc
Avj v s_ √ opjs
la r avlB, Dir Ad _r
bron. vlu

5

dr s_d Alo u
pam _C z du
Sp. hs n b rsv-, Intro DC
erp- l U u lau
plse hsb cpl crN
lru r atdc ln Pvj.

ls hs rzlt-n. sli
ncrs n sz vu ln.
p nl la r alC-Sam
recs ls laS acj, z
ev vpln- n pS, Intro DC z
lu Avj l rpa r ln
z qcl z psB. b du
so u rnu r f vlu
vu plse. _n u _c.
pam, Intro DC p rel r alC-
Sam _ u Cc. p ru
u plse No o Cc l
hlp s Pss u pam
qcl, _a e Aso rm
u la er A_ hpe l
asr qs + hlp n ne
_a ec, Dir Ad _r s_d.
du n hzla lcl r U=
fre No / ne b. cu

LESSON 32

1. Write a slightly raised and disjoined ᶫ for the word ending *ity* (pronounced *uh-tee*).

quality, q-l-ity qlᶫ

facilities, f-s-l-ity-s fslᶫˢ

possibility, p-s-bil-ity psBᶫ

authority, a-ith-r-ity alrᶫ

majority, m-j-r-ity jrᶫ

security, s-k-r-ity scrᶫ

2. Write ⋠ ⋡ to indicate parentheses.

Most of our staff (80%) have had their vacations.

8 vr Sf ⋠ 80% ⋡ vh lr vcjs.

BRIEF FORMS

able B

opinion opn

employ p

difficult dfc

contract kc

BRIEF FORM DEVELOPMENT

difficulty dfce

responsibility rspBᶫ

enable nB

ability Bᶫ

COMMONLY MISSPELLED WORDS

excellent

correspondence

YOUR BUSINESS VOCABULARY

term policy — In life insurance, a contract providing benefits for a limited number of years. It pays face value if the owner's death occurs during the time specified in the contract.

PRINCIPLES SUMMARY

1. Write for the word ending *ity (uh-tee)*: quality, q-l-ity
2. Write to indicate parentheses.

WORD DEVELOPMENT

Write the shorthand outlines for the following related words.

employ	-s ______	-ed ______	-ment ______
secure	-d ______	-ing ______	-ity ______
deduct	-s ______	-ible ______	-ibility ______
contract	-ed ______	-s ______	-ing ______
suit	-ed ______	-able ______	-ability ______

WORD CONSTRUCTION

Practice writing these words.

community, com-n-ity ______

capacity, k-p-s-ity ______

personality, per-s-n-l-ity ______

quantities, q-nt-ity-s ______

locality, l-k-l-ity ______

electricity, electr-s-ity ______

necessity, n-s-s-ity ______

probability, prah-b-bil-ity ______

eligibility, e-l-j-bil-ity ________ possibilities, p-s-bil-ity-s ________

WRITING ASSIGNMENT

Self-dictate the following letter as you write it in your shorthand notebook.

Gentlemen:

As the head of this hospital, I was happy to hear that a new children's unit is being proposed.[1] As part of this proposal, parents will be allowed to remain here in the hospital with their children.[2] Generally, such an arrangement provides a great benefit to the parents as well as the patients.

To determine[3] a need for this unit, a survey was made with local residents. Of the total surveyed, 80 percent were[4] in favor of this unit. I feel happy and proud to see this matter finally receiving the attention[5] it needs. As members of the hospital board, you will no doubt wish to receive a full report on this new plan.[6] Very truly yours, (124)

READING AND WRITING EXERCISES

1

dr bSr ls, l
kfr r fn kvrsj
ksrn c kc u Ar v
jrs bron, gi
Nca- erlr, (Intro DC) r bron
hs dsd- l rsl c
prp + hs p- e
bc c arms f h, c
Ppz- nu ors +
l PCs, eqle +

as c bsc kc no
n efc, p nl la c
flo Cnys r Ub d:
c nu ln ra l rpls
c ra pd orynll, el
Srl O . nu 10=yr
ln, p asc u alrne
l drap c nu agrem
bz Cnys, el rvu
bf clz, f c agrem
rqs. Ul SC, (Intro DC) c nu

ors l ac la rspBl,
iap u hlp n kp r
nu kc. ul

2

d-rs An lgf L, (Series)
cpes v kc, (Series) + rla-
lgl inf ksrn r sl
v prp. iz dli-lhr
la r clz lc pls z
scyl-ol qs or
dfces v ne cM, i
-s lcl u all l r
enc-cpes v cor
csl r orynl fr ins
plse o la hos. iv
n yl rsv- ne f
r nu ors Nca la
ly v lcn ol . nu
plse. d ub B ldl
la Aql cvry hsb
ar-x, h Aso rel
u cpe vr agrem

-C e sn-zu rqS-.
i as- uc no rec
r dd + ks r kc
kp-, lqs aq fu hlp.
cu

3

d ed h p-lsa lb
vzl Usq evn snr
ln e vpc-, i pln l
brq r nu sls-yrs
o . lrp lru r Wrn
plNs du r -c v
Mr 6. i -M l so
h r lM fslls +
Pgs crNl n efc.
el arv o fli 519 /
5 30p- o Wd. cd u
-e s + v dnr -
s la evn x, idap
-e Th -rn -u, (Series)
r nu -pes, (Series) + ne i
els u lq ly sd -e,

Intro DC

if s n l dfc l ar, ed, Dir Ad idlc r gSs lq lru a v plNs. e ...i ks c psBl v rN . bs f Th afnn. ...I du u lq? u opns a kb grl l r efls, e pln l lv / ab 9° c nx ...rn. u hlp, Slnl ap-. s

4

ds as ls L, n rsp lu rsN nqe re aplm rNls. alo ev no aplms avlB no, Intro DC e alspa opn ...n c nx 3 ...os. l ncry u lcp Cc ... s, edu rq . scr l dpzl w ad v . f ...os rN. ls dpzl lb ret- af u frnt vb r ...v- + . nspc sos la no dys v ocr-. e aso rqS 30 ds nls ...n u pln l ...v f c aplm, u ...a Cz . 1=yr or 2=yr ls. c 2=yr kc ofrs c avj v sv apxl 20$ P ...o n rN. eC unl klns kp lNre + cCn fsl^ls, elb hpe l so u . aplm. cl r rNl ofs l sl p . apym. su

5

dr lsn hr, c rpl u rqS-. z uc Intro DC se, u ern por, u ...S ...pl asl. e

agre lau lf ins
plse sd Pvd f
ejcj + dl nds vu
fl w evN vu dl,
l dz / lc l ⌒e
lz gls. e rcm lau
ins ofs bnfls v pl
6 sû P ern, i suq
u PCs · 20 = yr lr

plsew a l v 250T$.
r lB o pj 7 lSs
r bnfls + cSs v ls
sp pln. if u ⌒
Intro DC
l PCs r plse, s pl
kp + rel r enc-
aplc, lgf alo s
Dir Ad
l Avz u, ⌒ r lsn.
vlu

LESSON 33

1. Write *u* for the word beginning *un*.

until, un-t-l *utl*

unfair, un-f-r *ufr*

unpaid, un-p-d *upd*

unchanged, un-chay-n-j-duh *uCnj-*

unless, un-l-s *uls*

uncover, un-k-v-r *ucvr*

BRIEF FORM DEVELOPMENT

Use this principle to develop words from brief forms and abbreviations.

unable *uB*

unfortunate *ufCnt*

unsatisfactory *usat*

unnecessary *unes*

MORE ABOUT PHRASING

An easily recognized word may be omitted from common phrases or compound words. In the following examples, the shorthand outline for the italicized word has been omitted.

never*the*less *nvrls*

time *to* time *tt*

none*the*less *nnls*

up *to* date *pda*

USE COMMAS WITH APPOSITIVES.

An appositive is a word or group of words that explains, renames, or identifies someone or something that immediately precedes it in the sentence.

Appositives are usually set off by commas from the rest of the sentence. The following are examples of appositives:

□ His new textbook, *Business English*, has now been published.
□ Please see our sales manager, Sally Stanfield.
□ Mr. Ronald Jackson, the Secretary of State, will deliver our commencement address.

Appositives will be highlighted in the Reading and Writing Exercises by the abbreviation **Ap**.

YOUR BUSINESS VOCABULARY

computer terminal kpur trml — A device usually consisting of a keyboard and a screen that is used to input data to and output data from a computer. Also called a work station.

questionnaire qr — A set of questions assembled for the purpose of making a survey.

PRINCIPLES SUMMARY

1. Write u for the word beginning *un*: until, un-t-l utl.

WORD DEVELOPMENT

Write the shorthand outlines for the following related words.

able B	en- ______	dis- ______	un- ______
bound boN	re- ______	un- ______	-ary ______
bend bN	-s ______	-ing ______	un- ______
cover cvr	-ed ______	-ing ______	un- ______
willing l	-ly ______	-ness ______	un- ______

WORD CONSTRUCTION

Practice writing these words.

unlike, un-l-k ______

unreasonable, un-re-z-n-ble ______

unearned, un-e-r-n-duh ______

unloaded, un-l-d-ed ______

uncut, un-k-t __________	unlisted, un-l-st-ed __________
undivided, un-d-v-d-ed __________	unemployed, un-employ-duh __________
undue, un-d-u __________	unwelcome, un-wel-come __________

WRITING ASSIGNMENT

Self-dictate the following memo as you write it in your shorthand notebook.

MEMO TO: Manager of Boy's Wear

We will offer savings of between 20 and 30 percent on all[1] back-to-school needs—clothing, as well as supplies. All clothing should be marked down 20 percent. All school supplies will be[2] displayed between the boy's and girl's departments.

We will accept payment in the form of cash, credit cards, and personal[3] checks. Those persons wishing to cash payroll checks should be sent to the credit office. All personal checks should be[4] seen by the department manager.

We suggest your clerks remind all shoppers that clothing items may be returned[5] within one week following the purchase. (107)

READING AND WRITING EXERCISES

1

mo l -r Sf r
so ls yr z r bS
ev E h, r Pdcs
-d. fvrB -pry +
e rsv- me kplms
af r so, e Aso
rsv- s- suggs.

f ex me dlrs r v
opn la. 60=d dle
L, l lq. r sdb
rds- l 30 ds. f r
A psB el -c la Cny
-n r nx fu -os,
ag r kplms rsv-
- loz rf- l r Dpla

v c ras kc- l
kpur lrmls. eh
apxl 1M$ rl v
dse lr, r pes
aso d . q pry.
r snsr lqs q l .
olSN Sff.v so.

2

drs clrc i N
u lno la v bk .
sr ak ajN f nyl
lf inc, z v Ma i
l v l . nu lcq /
819 S Sa S r l
ku lgv u Psnl Svs
nE und /, n od
l brq u plse pda
v enc- . qr asc
f sp inf. d u p
rel / f v pSy =
fre env Pvd-x, p
nl la i Ufn No

(555-3100) r ns
uCny-. ull Ma i uc
vzl e / i P ofs.
if uv qs, (Intro DC) hp ul
cl. n ur v nbrh, (Intro DC)
Sp b. i asSN +
i r a gld l lc
u. uvl

3

d rdr ev ar sN
sv bls f r gzn, (Ap)
arl nz, (Ap) od- n u n.
so fr ev n rsv- ne
pam or plny, / n
r cS l asc f pams
u ods. e lq r rdrs
ap / kv v b B lc
pams nE ly sll
lr ol hoshld or ofs
aks. e ks r rdrs lb
nf- Nvs hu ac
rspBl f kcs ly v

d, eno la lr ,
. q rzn fu dla n
rc pam, / l lc ol
. fu mts l stl ls
lr = elr ⌣ . Cc
or . fu rds vpln
(dla, p rel u
rsp ⌣ (inv w
aco env, su

4

d dvd lqf opl l
rcm u assN yr, **Ap**
jnfr yq, f pzj **Ap**
v pb rljs drs, idu
so ⌣ plzr, jnfr hs
me fn ql ls rep v q
ym, 1 Srq py, hr
B L l vprs hr opns bo
n spC + n ri, se
sos . USN v co gls
alq ⌣ . snsr ksrn
f r ol pes, jnfr

as s f rspB L f ne
jb no lr ho dfc,
ull se k l (Av
dpl, **Intro DC** jnfr h no vp
n ym, nvrls se
Svz- sv Pjcs w
mr v . vp- dpl
hd, n u opn jnfr
, rde f ncrs- rspB L,
se l brq me fn ql ls
l (pzj U ksj, ul

5

dK er kvrl u bl l
. nu elnc dla Pss
sl C l Sv u
efsNl, hr r (
bsc Cnjs afc u
ln pams:, 1, z v
Ja 1 el p (us v
enc- pam bc, 2,
u nu ol du da l
A b (frS d v eC

~o. if u pam z
Intro DC
du o Ja 10, s no
du o Ja1. / lb du
r fr8 d v E ~o
lraf, 3. if u pams
r at—lcl ddc-f
Intro DC
u Cc or sv ak, ul
n rsv . pam bc,
lz Cnjs l nB s l
Pss u pams — P—ll.
Intro DC
if uv qs, p cl / bq-
ofs nr8 u or r K
Svs dpl. cu

LESSON 34

1. Write sl for the sound of *shul* and the word ending *chul* (cial, tial).

official, o-f-ish-l ofsl
special, s-p-ish-l spsl
initial, i-n-ish-l insl
financial, f-n-n-ish-l fnnsl
potential, p-t-n-ish-l ptnsl
social, s-ish-l ssl

ABBREVIATIONS

volume vol
literature lil
America, American a

BRIEF FORMS

develop dv
organize og
success suc
standard Sd
acknowledge ac
associate aso
congratulate kg

BRIEF FORM DEVELOPMENT

acknowledgment acjm
organizations ogjs
organizing og
standards Sds
associations asojs
development dvm
congratulations kgjs
developing dv

COMMONLY MISSPELLED WORDS

cites sis

questionnaire qr

YOUR BUSINESS VOCABULARY

group retirement plan grp rtrm pln — A plan to provide income for retired employees; premiums may be paid entirely by the employer or partly by the employer and partly by the employee.

accordingly acrdl — Within (according to) a special way.

PRINCIPLES SUMMARY

1. Write sl for the sound of *shul* and the word ending *chul* (cial, tial): official, o-f-ish-l ofsl ; financial, f-n-n-ish-l fnnsl.

WORD DEVELOPMENT

Write the shorthand outlines for the following related words.

initial insl	-s ______	-ed ______	-ly ______
social ssl	-s ______	-ly ______	-ize ______
special spsl	-s ______	-ly ______	-ize ______
develop dv	-s ______	-ed ______	-ments ______
acknowledge acj	-d ______	-s ______	-ments ______

WORD CONSTRUCTION

Practice writing these words.

commercial, com-r-ish-l ______

officially, o-f-ish-l-ly ______

essential, e-s-n-ish-l ______

financially, f-n-n-ish-l-ly ______

potentially, p-t-n-ish-l-ly ______

residential, r-z-d-n-ish-l ______

sequential, s-q-n-ish-l ______

developer, develop-r ______

associated, associate-d ______

congratulating, congratulate-ing ______

WRITING ASSIGNMENT

Self-dictate the following letter as you write it in your shorthand notebook.

Dear Senator Martin:

As you know, some members of our group have been involved in a fight to prevent increases[1] in oil and gasoline rates. We invite you to help by voting to defeat this gasoline bill.

This bill would[2] allow companies to determine their own rates. It would also provide new policies for locating oil on[3] properties near the sea. Those new policies could be very damaging to a great number of people in many[4] ways. We hope that you will join our cause. Help us win this fight. Yours truly, (92)

READING AND WRITING EXERCISES

1

d pl i [illegible] l vprs
[illegible] i spl f nu bns
ssh ofsll adpl-s
dpll [illegible]e, r sls
Psnl v dvo- [illegible]C
[illegible] l dv- . dm f r
Pdc + rzlls vb
lM, z r [illegible] cvr
Intro DC
kus l gro, ods ncrs
acrdl, af P- c nu
plse c r rynl sls
kvn i rsv- me cls

f sls Psnl ksrn-
pys ly foN kfz- n
od l PvN MUSN i
pln l isu . mo ri
a a vpln- c plse n
dll, z . insl Sp n
oq- . [illegible]e [illegible] a sls
yrs lq O eC py,
d ub B l jyn s nx
Fr / 10 a [illegible] x, a n
a c Ppzl hsb l
rsv- m fld, i vpc
lse evn grr suc n

nyl sls. su

2

ddr lys / gvs
e gr saly l rcm
dr elzbl crlr f rq
v aso Pfsr. z spl
f ls acj i ofr c alC-
fl kln . sre v hr
vp. Aso d 2
arlcls se rsNl
pbls- alq opns
v SdNs + ol fclle,
elzbl jyn- r Sf 3
yrs aq. se hs dv-
nu crss n A hSre
C v kb- C l r
Pq. se sos . re f hi
lC Sds + Pvds .
lN ex f SdNs +
ol fclle, elzbl .
lCr gr plnsl +
. Ps fCr. / ss

ol apo lae acj hr
kbjs ls Pq.
vlu

3

drs clrc idlc l
lqf e e o
Mn l Dcs pm
SC. Alo ih aq- s
lil o ho l aprC
Intro DC
plnsl prs, u Avs
z v spsl hlp. i no
ap fl c pl v.
c . q pry + w
. blr USN v ho l
ak la gl, flo u
Avs + ri Nv Ls
v aplcj lsN
eC cpe v rza.
i Aso ap c rza
u gv e. dv
o rza ez
+ suc ln ih vpc-.

z · rzlt vr e l
no fl la ic c
la insl klc ·
kfdN + Pfyl q,
lqu aq fu hlp.
ul

4

dr prcr lqu, (Dir Ad) r
prcr, (Dir Ad) f kp r qr
ksrn / ssl scr'
rf bl. hr r s
rzlls f la Sva:,
1. / yr' v ppl Sva-
€ 82% € rli po X
nk l nln lr Sd
v lv, 2. / n srs
v nk af rlrm ks
f grp plns Pvd-
b prs + lbr ogjs.
ol srss ls-
Psnl bs or prp, (Series)
ins dvdNs, (Series) + Psnl

sv, 3. S ppl
agre- la ssl scr'
bnflsaln r n sfsN
l e fnnsl dms
pz- b nflq, 4. apxl
33% Sa- la · nu Pq
sdb dv- l rpls /
S pln, lqu aq f
pp n Sva. ul

5

dr dvdsn kgjs
r n od fu + u fl.
u n hsb slc- f
nx vol v yq ppl
n A, (Ap) · v spsl
pbq, ls Dlg-
bc lss Nvs U / aq
v 40 hu r ern
olSN rcgnq. / sis
/ sucs v yq ppl
n A cs v lf=bs, (Series)
N, (Series) ejcq, (Series) gvl, (Series) spls, (Series)

Series

la, + —dsn, (enc-
dla se sps Psnl
+ Pfjl inf lb d- n
r nx vol. p rd +

rel (inf — ne
crcjs u — + Lc,
aq kgjs o rsv ls
spsl aw. cu

LESSON 35

RECAP AND REVIEW

1. In Lessons 29–34, you learned to write the following word beginnings:

extr and extra X

aks, eks, iks, oks, uks, eggs \

un u

2. These word endings were presented:

bil, ble *(bul)*, or bly B

ity *(uh-tee)* l

cial, tial *(shul, chul)* sl

3. These words illustrate all of the new principles studied in Lessons 29–34:

accident, x-d-nt \dN

long, l-ong lg

facilities, f-s-l-ity-s fsl ls

exciting, x-ite-ing \i_

exist, x-st \S

until, un-t-l utl

double, d-ble dB

relaxing, re-l-x-ing rlx_

extremely, extr-m-ly Xml

effect, e-f-k efc

financial, f-n-n-ish-l fnnsl

social, s-ish-l ssl

4. You learned to indicate time in the following way:

one o'clock 1°

11:30 a.m. 11^{30}a

12 noon 12 nn

10:30 p.m. 10^{30}p

5. Easily recognized words are omitted from common phrases:

nevertheless nvrls time *to* time tt

none*the*less nnls up *to* date pda

6. Transcribe the following abbreviations:

vol lit a

7. How quickly can you write these brief forms?

always ____	prove ____	immediate ____
consider ____	next ____	note ____
experience ____	already ____	approximate ____
able ____	opinion ____	difficult ____
contract ____	employ ____	standard ____
develop ____	organize ____	associate ____
acknowledge ____	success ____	congratulate ____

READING AND WRITING EXERCISES

1

dS hr r 4 rzns y usd cp rd, 1. ur . ejca- Psn, 2. uno . brgn -n u se /, 3. u blv n sv me -n uc, 4. uno ho

l lc avy v . rr opl, uf und . 5l rzn ks ls. ur a-q ol 1H ppl lrsv ls ofr. z pl v . rr -r Pq u + 99 ols vb slc- l lrn vcj hrs, vlj hrs

, . pln- nbrh Ar
U kSrcj. , Pfc f
yq fls. vlj hs
hs E ul N + .
n u se r kcs la
r avlB, ul PbB sa
u cN afd n l b! ,
ll s pv , . njy
fre ni + f u o opns.
Lc u rzrvj rel r
enc- nl . b hre= r
ofr Ns nx o.
rzrv u da l.
cu

Intro DC

rqS-. ufCnll r
scl dz n N ull
Ma 25. a l bgn
r flo Mn Ma 28
P ll / 8 a , lc
fw l ls opl l lrn,
gro, + bld nu scls.
ufl Sln r pzj l
brg me nu + v
vps, lqf c ls
opl psB. uls l hr
dfrNl, l rpl lu
ofs 6 rn v Ma
28. cu

Series

Series

Intro DC

2

ds rbrls hpe
l ac r pzj v ex
sec u fr. l ks
/ . Clnj lb r Psn
Czn f rspBls u
dS-, ldb dli- l bgn
pm o Ma 21 zu

3

ds bxls lqf nqe.
ublv r enc- lil l
asr u qs, E Dr
ps . f= L Svzr
hu cs sr la r
Psnl r fl lrn- n
Svs r elnc lprus.

r Drs sl p lrn sjs
f Sf, (Series) dlrs, (Series) + Ks apxl
3 s Pyr, E Dr ,
eqp- ⌣ / nre
+ l8 eqpm nd- l
rpr r ns. uf /
dz bk nes l od pls
f / fclre, (Intro DC) loz ods
r Pss- + - l, uf
udlc frlr inf, (Intro DC) r
bxlz, (Dir Ad) p klc e aq.
efl r lrn , v vlu
n ol l nu pes b
Aso l ku Psnl z
l. er A gld l asr
u qs. su

4

1 s la v yr
n e pl a a lrs
v ofs l r Psnl
ps ⌣ fl + frNs.
z . kc K u Ar no

la r Sf kus s 24=
hr Pq du / X s
hlds. n od l alo
r pes z C Psnl
z psB e Alr r
Av + Pq scjls f .
fu ds. f 8 p Dc 23
ull 8 a Dc 26 el
Pvd lp- Pq. A Av
lb brdcS bln loz
das sdb dl- l r
ofss b 5 p Dc 20
l alo sfN f
prprj, a e Aso
lc ls opl l lqf
plrny. ev nyy-Sv
u du / pS yr + lc
fw l ku r rljs. cu

5

d frNs n r grp
es aq nx o, (Intro DC)
el lk slg clrg z

gl spcr. r ~e,
b ~v- bc , ~c l
Mr 8. sle z uB l
alN o d rglrl
scjl- f ~e, sle
, lrcgnz- n r
sle. se hs hd-
me ~pl ks. ~S
rsNl se z elc-
P v C~br v krs,
sle ks l s ~l
flo. lrp abrd +
se brgs v nz.

lrvl o bhf vr sle
sle ~d ~ apxl 45
corps. Alo r ~
z . lq + dfc , Intro DC
Pds- lN rzlls.
ev Ar rsv- ~rd
la , co plns lsN
. rep hr l nvSga
bld . nu plN,
p nl r Cnj ou
clNrs + pln lb
P f ~e. vlu

Transcribing Shorthand Notes

When you transcribe shorthand notes, your goal is to produce an attractive printed document that speaks well of you, your supervisor, and your business.

The following step-by-step procedures provide an efficient, reliable method of producing the perfect transcript.

BEFORE BEGINNING TO TYPE OR KEYBOARD

1. Determine the order in which each document should be completed. Which one should be done first, second, and so on? Then transcribe each document according to its order of priority.
2. Determine the letter style, the format, and the margin settings for each document.
3. Verify the spellings of any words that you are not certain of by checking a dictionary. Learn to watch for commonly misspelled words that often slip by unnoticed.
4. Elevate your notepad for convenient reading before beginning to type or keyboard.

BEFORE PRINTING OR REMOVING THE DOCUMENT

1. Proofread carefully—not once, but twice. Read first against your notes to be certain that your copy is complete and accurate; then read again for typographical, spelling, punctuation, or grammatical errors you might have overlooked.

2. Make any necessary corrections before you print the document if you are using a word processor or while the document is in the machine if you are using a typewriter.

BEFORE PRESENTING THE DOCUMENT FOR SIGNATURE

1. Draw a line through the shorthand notes that you have transcribed to indicate that you no longer need them.
2. Look at your transcript carefully. Is it attractively arranged on the page? Does it contain noticeable corrections? When your transcribed copy is neat, free of errors, and shows no evidence of correction, it is ready to be signed and mailed.
3. Type the envelope, giving it the same careful attention you gave the letter.
4. If the letter calls for enclosures, assemble them now to be presented with the letter.
5. Present the document for your supervisor's signature, submitting the envelope and any specified enclosures along with the transcript.

A WORD ABOUT EQUIPMENT AND SUPPLIES

Some supplies and procedures will vary slightly depending upon the printing equipment that you use. However, you should always have the following items at your work station:

1. a dictionary
2. a list of commonly misspelled words
3. a secretarial procedures manual
4. an English usage manual

Electric or electronic typewriters usually provide correcting features. Word processors allow you to make corrections in the copy displayed on the video screen before the document is printed. If your machine does not have a correcting feature, choose the most effective agent available—correction film, tape, or fluid. Master the use of the correcting agent so that your transcript will not show any sign of correction.

LESSON 36

1. Write *n* for the sounds of *ance, ence, nce,* and *nse* (pronounced *ence*).

dance, d-nce dn
balance, b-l-nce bln
expense, x-p-nse xpn
agency, a-j-nce-e ajne
since, s-nce sn
defense, d-f-nse dfn
advance, ad-v-nce avn
efficiency, e-f-ish-nce-e efshne

2. Write s for the word beginning *sub.*

submit, sub-m-t s-mt
subscribe, sub-scribe sS
subscription, sub-scrip-tion sSp
subway, sub-w-a s-wa
substantial, sub-st-n-ish-l sSnshl
subject, sub-j-k sjc

PHRASES

that you are laur
that you will laul

COMMONLY MISSPELLED WORDS

congratulate kq
already ar

YOUR BUSINESS VOCABULARY

unpaid balance — The total amount of money remaining to be paid on a bill or loan.

PRINCIPLES SUMMARY

1. Write [shorthand] for the sound of *ance, ence, nce, nse*: dance, d-nce [shorthand].
2. Write [shorthand] for the word beginning *sub*: submit, sub-m-t [shorthand].

WORD DEVELOPMENT

Write the shorthand outlines for the following related words.

accept	-ed ______	-ing ______	-ance ______
subject	-ed ______	-s ______	-ing ______
assist	-ed ______	-ing ______	-ance ______
submit	-ted ______	-s ______	-ting ______
accord	-ed ______	-ing ______	-ance ______

WORD CONSTRUCTION

Practice writing these words.

chance, chay-nce ______	confidence, con-f-d-nce ______
density, d-nse-ity ______	remittance, re-m-t-nce ______
evidence, e-v-d-nce ______	performance, per-for-m-nce ______
instance, in-st-nce ______	substandard, sub-standard ______
finance, f-n-nce ______	subcommittee, sub-committee ______

WRITING ASSIGNMENT

Self-dictate the following letter as you write it in your shorthand notebook.

Dear Ms. Jackson:

Thank you for your answer to my letter. The booklets you sent will greatly help me in doing a[1] research paper due this term.

I anticipate finishing the paper in two weeks. The only problem I've had[2] is obtaining data from companies located out of town. Out of a total of seven, I have heard from[3] only four. I am now waiting for responses from the remaining three before analyzing the final[4] results.

You will certainly receive a copy of my finished report. Yours truly, (94)

READING AND WRITING EXERCISES

1

drs sd ev
rzrv- . efsNe
aplm fu n lq bC.
c aplm hs . lN
vu v oq + A v fsl^ls
u rqS-, sN u vq
fls du c bze szn, (Intro DC)
e rcm lau kfr u
rzrvq. / db z
lcl , c n AvN,
p sN . 50$ dpzl
no l rzrv ls
aplm. ef u s
l hNl A arms fu, (Intro DC)
elb hpe l fw u
Cc. el Aso kfr c
das vu Sa, efl
Sln laul nyy lv
n ls Cr aplm
o bC. lqf alo s
l asSu n c u
lrvl plns. cu

2

mo l A dpl hds
p nl la U bjl e
l bgn erl nx yr.
s pl lau sd u
Ppz- bjls b Ja 6.

insl me l bgn
md. fnl apvl,
scjl- f N v Ap,
bcz v lrj cls n Sa
aloNs usd mc E
efl l rds pNs.
sN no nu fN,
Intro DC
avlB, / lb psB
l bgn nu Pgs.
ino laur A du u
bS lcp pNs don,
me vu v asc- ab
pa ncrss. er sug
. Sd 7% ncrs f A
Psnl, ne adjl rqSs
f fN mS b rvu- bf
Api. eap u hlp n
Pvd u bjl rqSs
zz psB.

3

dS i rd w apj
u insl isu v bs
rvu + wS l od 3
sSjs lb gvn z Xms
gfls. m enc
ms + adrss fu
us, i wS l lc Av
vu Xms Dk. m
enc . Cc f lol
amt v 35^{85}. ls sd
cvr A hNl fes, zu
Intro DC
USN / ul md . gre
crd anoN gfl.
l crd arv bf
Xms, p sN me
kfrj la gfl
crds vb md-.
lqu v mC. ul

4

d sr n. fu wcs ul
pl a a fnl ms +
bgn . nu lf, l
acj mpl v ls
evN ev asc- mr

Ap Ap
dvd cx, sec v Sa,
l dl r kNm adrs.
l r dli r cx hs ac->
n, brf ls n ofs
r cx hs pv- lb.
olSN ldr. efl fCnl
lv ls opl lhr h. ehp
hl +r, drs f. nu
bgn ag nys, ls, c
lS L l ru l S vu.
zu UP, +l kq u
+lqf spl. a ub
Series
rw- c bS v hll,
Series
. Sla crr, + saly
v akm. abv a nyy
u nu lf. su

5

drs bxlr edlc l
rm u lau ak,
pS du. d u lc.
ml no l l s.
Cc, f l e a
Olc. pam. sN uv
Intro DC
a pd u bls o l,
er Sln ls dla S
b c rzll v. Osi.
if ls, s ol rzn
Intro DC
y ev n hrd f u,
d u drp s. nl v
plny, Ph esd py
ol aq laul sv me
b s l u pams n
avN. n u pam
Intro DC
arvs la,. fe, G-
aq c upd blN,
lqf all l ls dr.
if u pam, ar n
Intro DC
l,p Dre ls nls.
su

LESSON 37

1. Write **v** for the medial or final sound of *tive*.

active, a-k-tive acv

effective, e-f-k-tive efcv

selective, s-l-k-tive slcv

relative, r-l-tive rlv

objective, o-b-j-k-tive objcv

positive, p-z-tive pzv

Write these additional words:

actively acvl

activity acv

relatively rlvl

effectiveness efcv

BRIEF FORMS

usual uz

work, world

manufacture

signature, significant, significance sig

BRIEF FORM DEVELOPMENT

usually uzl

unusual uuz

working

manufacturer

manufacturing

PHRASES

I appreciate iap

to work

that I tai

USE COMMAS WITH PARENTHETICAL EXPRESSIONS.

A parenthetical expression is a word or group of words that interrupts the natural flow of the sentence. These expressions are often used to add emphasis or show contrast. When removed from the sentence, such expressions do not change the meaning of the sentence.

When the word or phrase occurs in the middle of the sentence, place a comma before and after the expression. If the expression occurs at the beginning or end of the sentence, use only one comma. Some common examples of parenthetical expressions are as follows:

as a rule	furthermore
in other words	for instance
for example	of course
on the other hand	in fact
therefore	however
naturally	nevertheless

- □ We will be happy, *however,* to send you the fabric we have in stock.
- □ We do not, *as a rule,* accept cash payments for merchandise.
- □ Trust funds offer excellent tax benefits, *for example.*

In following lessons, parenthetical expressions will be highlighted by the abbreviation **Paren**.

YOUR BUSINESS VOCABULARY

job satisfaction — jb saty — Degree of contentment an employee feels toward his or her employment position.

PRINCIPLES SUMMARY

1. Write v for the medial or final sound of *tive*: active, a-k-tive acv.

WORD DEVELOPMENT

Write the shorthand outlines for the following related words.

object obyc	-ed ______	-s ______	-tive ______
effect efc	-s ______	-tive ______	-tively ______
act ac	-ed ______	-tion ______	-tive ______

work [shorthand] -s ________ -ed ________ -er ________

collect clc -s ________ -tion ________ -tive ________

WORD CONSTRUCTION Practice writing these words.

productivity, pro-d-k-tive-ity ________

protective, pro-t-k-tive ________

activities, a-k-tive-ity-s ________

defective, d-f-k-tive ________

effectiveness, e-f-k-tive-ness ________

sensitive, s-nse-tive ________

informative, in-for-m-tive ________

worldly, world-ly ________

attractive, a-t-r-k-tive ________

workshop, work-ish-p ________

WRITING ASSIGNMENT Self-dictate the following letter as you write it in your shorthand notebook.

Dear Mrs. Gibson:

Our shipments have been arriving after the due date. Our May package was due on the 3rd but[1] was received on the 9th. Our June and July shipments arrived nearly two weeks late.

This problem may have been caused by[2] our recent move. Our letter of April 2 asked you to delay the May shipment while we were getting situated[3] in the new building. Perhaps we did not say when to resume shipping at the regular date. You have our[4] apologies for the misleading message.

We now wish to return to the old schedule. Yours truly, (98)

READING AND WRITING EXERCISES

1

mo l a dpl yrs z uz (Paren) eC vu lb asc- l Ppr . Pf M rpl o Nv pes. hoE (Paren) ls yrs rpl lb dfrM.

z uc se f (alC-
Intro DC
cpe, el asc pes lr
Series
opns re lr o Pdcv,
Series
jb salj, + crr gls, p
ncrj u ppl l kp lz
rpls z acrll z psB.
b Sln la E, USNs
(Pps v rpl=la s
l hlp eC Psn aCv
, or hr gls, (rzlts
v lz rpls l v . sig
efc o fCr pln. b
o lglr el ncrs (
efsNe vr ogj.

2

dr srp , Slnl
Ap
njy- rd (mS,
nu dvms n rd
Pss. lqf alo e
lse (Sde n AvN.
p- lofr opns
o s efcv', , ks ls

o Lb . sig kbj l
(fld. r evns
gvs s . uuz lc (
fCr + s pc o ofs
Psjrs. z h Sa- w
Intro DC
frS Cplr, , objcvs
r l Sva Sd eqpm
n us ld + dS Pdcs
sn Lb avlB, r
evns , slcv n , Cys
v exs + brf n , dSjs.
Series
, foN (ri Lb clr,
Series Paren
l oq, + efcv, aq,
,ap (opl Lo u
n rvu ls Sde. p cl
o e if ,cb v frlr
hlp. cu

3

d ed no la A lS ,
Intro DC
kp, er alrz (rls v
. nu Pdc. efcv
Paren
l, el f njns f

sl arcrft zlz
r apo nSl, eqpm,
e rsv- ofsl nls ls
rn l rls r Pdc
f N a r, p Cn,
u recs l so r flo
crcjs. e a- . nu
spl sS + asn- .
nu cd No l rflc
r Cn, n prs, ods
lb s- n . xm
v 60 ds. e a se .
slo Srl n sls du
l Pbls n arcrft
Paren
N. hoE, e pc sig
ncrss du r frS 18
os. ehp l ld r
r n 5 yrs, p
ll e no if uv
ne qs. su

4

d G K n , . Nr

sl n jS . ord sl.
Intro DC
n u se r Dk prss,
ul no. e rrl ofr sv
lc lz. ln e c avlB
ol l v spsl ppl=
r G Ks, ls , n . av-
sl. r . Psnl nvl,
l r rglr Ks l nj,
spsl bnfls. p ks
r r a v sa lqf
plrn, Cz f r lp
Series
frs= erl a,
Series
lrdyl, + kl prre
clcjs. jyn s f cfe +
broz lru r nu arl
Dplas. ucd b r nr
v . prz lb gvn aa
eC d, sp r , vr kv
lcjs ld + sv. rmbr
la cs , n nes. u
sig l rzrv r ls
vu Cys. su

5

d hnre e rsNl
nvr- . prl o ri bs
Ls l lC . crs n r
plN, se Srs- la . q
L, dr + brf, - inf
sdb l oq- , – C f
unes kNs, lz c Dlrc
- rdr, iz – prs- b hr
Avs lcp - ln vr Ls
pzv, ec evn sa no
n . pzv – a, uc se
lai foN ls crs lb
X–l – pl, d u lc
lhr – ab sC .
crs fu ofs, , idb
hpe l rf u l - nSrcr,
i frl blv la ec A
bnfl f– sC nSrcq,
vlu

LESSON 38

1. Write *f* for the word ending *ful*.

useful, u-s-ful *usf*

careful, k-r-ful *crf*

carefully, k-r-ful-ly *crfl*

wonderful, w-nd-r-ful *Nrf*

helpful, h-l-p-ful *hlpf*

thankful, ith-ank-ful *Lqf*

Write *f* also for the word ending *ify* (pronounced *uh-fi*).

certify, cer-t-ify *Slf*

justify, j-st-ify *jSf*

qualify, q-l-ify *qlf*

classify, k-l-s-ify *clsf*

2. Write *f1* for the word ending *ification*.

classification, k-l-s-ification *clsf1*

identification, i-d-nt-ification *idNf1*

qualification, q-l-ification *qlf1*

modifications, m-d-ification-s *dfs*

BRIEF FORM DEVELOPMENT

Use these principles to form new words from brief forms:

successful *sucf*

notification *nlf1*

notify *nlf*

grateful *grf*

COMMONLY MISSPELLED WORDS

cannot cn

benefited bnfl-

YOUR BUSINESS VOCABULARY

deductible ddcB In reference to insurance policies, a set amount of money to be paid by the policyholder toward the total amount of damages on any claim.

PRINCIPLES SUMMARY

1. Write f for the word endings *ful* and *ify* (uh-fi): useful, u-s-ful usf; notify, note-ify nlf.
2. Write f1 for the word ending *ification*: qualification, q-l-ification qlf1.

WORD DEVELOPMENT

Write the shorthand outlines for the following related words.

wonder Nr	-ed ______	-ing ______	-ful ______
use us	-less ______	-ful ______	-fulness ______
help hlp	-ing ______	-ful ______	-fulness ______
class cls	-ify ______	-ified ______	-ification ______
just jS	-ify ______	-ifies ______	-ification ______

WORD CONSTRUCTION

Practice writing these words.

identify, i-d-nt-ify ______	certification, cer-t-ification ______
qualified, q-l-ify-duh ______	forgetful, for-gay-t-ful ______
verify, v-r-ify ______	verification, v-r-ification ______
modify, m-d-ify ______	clarification, k-l-r-ification ______
unlawful, un-l-aw-ful ______	hopefully, h-p-ful-ly ______

WRITING ASSIGNMENT

Self-dictate the following letter as you write it in your shorthand notebook.

Dear Mrs. Billings:

Our nation's banks handle billions of dollars each year for millions of customers, but there is[1] no customer at our bank whom we value more than you. Enclosed is your bank receipt for the money you have asked[2] us to manage for you.

According to our agreement, we will make all your monthly payments while you are out of[3] town. When you return, we will provide you with a report indicating which bills we have paid. The report will also[4] show any earnings on your deposit here at our bank.

If you make arrangements to lease your apartment while[5] traveling, please be sure to send us a copy of the lease agreement. Please include the name of your attorney.[6] We want to be certain we have all the information we may need to manage your money well. Yours truly,[7] (140)

READING AND WRITING EXERCISES

1

drs dvdsn lqf
nlf- s Pdl ab r
ths lcn f u cro
Sp 5 / apxl 3 30 p >
af e vm- u plse, e (Intro DC)
dl- lau cvry Pvds
. 150$ ddcB f lss
sC zu dS. lr r pys
l r ddcB b ly uzl
ksrn dys rzll f
nCrl czs. u lss
cn b clsf- a nq l>
r recs so la r lol
vlu v ths lcn z
178$. lrf, er enc . (Paren)
Cc f 28$- f uv frlr
gs re ls dr, p fl (Intro DC)
fre lcl / ne l, er
a rde l pln u
plse + gv u r bs
Plcy ofr- b /. cu

2

ddr jfres i bnfl-
grl f- c inf cvr-
n u ak cls + Aso
f- c olsd Pjcs e
kp-, n- p- lsa la
w Ar b B l aplc
s- v la nlj, f 3
-os wb -o pl h
w ofs v . Slf- pb
akN, w asS- n
clsf- fnnsl dla z
pl v -i rspBts lr,
n- no Ppr . rz -a
+ Ls v aplcj, sN
ur l glf- l kN o
-i ejcjl bcgroN, Intro DC
-a i lS u n- z
. rfN, u rcmj
db v hlpf, vlu

bcll u rqS-, Ap cr f
psN , h- " ehp u
fN c pbj nf-v +
usf, -a e Aso rm
u v f hll cr Svs e
no ofr, e cre . kp
ln v hll cr eqpm
f us w h-, uc rN
ne ch- - no dpzl
rq-, u pa ol la pl v
pN n cvr- b u ins,
n -S css, Paren u ins
pas f E + rNl
eqpm cSs u nlq,
if uv qs ab u cvrj, Intro DC
Dcs h- - r Pfjl
Sf, ly r spslSs n
fl -dcl chs + lb
hpe lgv u asSN,
k l c prls f kv
Svs + bS v Pfjl
cr, -n ql' ks, Intro DC uc
k o s, ul

3

drs grgre hr, c

4

d nu pe lk l o
elncs. w enc-env
ulfN 3 ths v vlu
ou nu jb, frS, u
pe idNfj crd. p
A u sig + cre crd
du rglr o hrs. b
Ppr-l so u crd n
u k nl or lv bld,
sec th, u hll
bnfls bcll. rd
crfl. if uv ne qs
re u hsp or dNl
cvrj, (Intro DC) cl r Psnl ofs
nl, 3d th, (Ap) u
pe hNbc, (Ap) Pvds .
kp gd l r cos Svss
+ plses. p bk f lr
r Psjrs du u frS
c ou nu jb, if uv
ne qs, (Intro DC) dN hzla lcl
o s ne . su

5

d r edws u m z
sug-l e bcz vu
rSC n clsf- rr
plNs. d u p assS
s n c. idNfj v
enc- lf, cls
hsb clc lvs du
pS 2 cs. 1 v
SdNs brl n ls lf.
s n sn n ne v
bcs n r scl lbrre.
af e d. crf SC v
lcl w ke lbrre, (Intro DC) e
foN enc-flogrf
la lcs vcl lc r lf.
z uc se, (Intro DC) bo lvs v
s uuz sp.
hoE, (Paren) plN w
pcCr gros w Wrn
Sas + cd n psB
gro ls fr E. or cd
x, ehp uc idNf

r Dcvre, ls cls
Pjc hs bk · sig

lrn vp f E1, vlu

LESSON 39

1. Write a capital N for the word beginnings *enter, inter,* and *intro.*

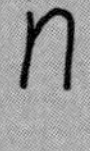

enterprise, enter-p-r-z Nprz

interest, inter-st NS

interview, inter-v-u Nvu

international, inter-n-tion-l Nnjl

introduced, intro-d-s-duh Nds-

introductory, intro-d-k-t-r-e Ndctre

2. Write sf for the word beginning and ending *self.*

self-addressed, self-a-d-r-s-duh sfadrs-

self-made, self-m-d sf‿d

self-confidence, self-con-f-d-nce sfkfdN

self-assurance, self-a-ish-r-nce sfasrN

himself, him-self hsf

herself, h-r-self hrsf

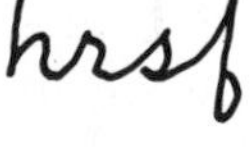

yourself, your-self usf

itself, it-self ‿sf

3. Write svs for the word ending *selves.*

ourselves, our-selves rsvs — yourselves, your-selves usvs

themselves, ith-m-selves]svs

ABBREVIATIONS

establish esl — superintendent S

BRIEF FORMS

circumstance Sk — once oN

particular plc — administrate am

control kl — sample sa

BRIEF FORM DEVELOPMENT

circumstances Sks — particularly plcl

circumstantial Sksl — administration amj

controlled kl- — samples sas

USE A COMMA TO SET OFF DATES IN SENTENCES.

When naming a day of the week, followed by the date, place a comma after the day of the week and the date. If the date falls at the end of the sentence, place a comma only after the day of the week.

- □ The meeting scheduled for Wednesday, April 2, has been postponed.
- □ The next board meeting will be held on Tuesday, March 7.

In following lessons, commas around dates will be highlighted in your Reading and Writing Exercises by the word **Date**.

YOUR BUSINESS VOCABULARY

international Nnjl — Having to do with activities that extend across national boundaries.

academic programs acdc Pgs — Specialized areas of study within a school curriculum.

PRINCIPLES SUMMARY

1. Write a capital *N* for the word beginnings *enter, inter,* and *intro*: interest, inter-st *Ns*.
2. Write *sf* for the word beginning and ending *self*: herself, h-r-self *hrsf*.
3. Write *svs* for the word ending *selves*: yourselves, your-selves *usvs*.

WORD DEVELOPMENT

Write the shorthand outlines for the following related words.

entertain *Ntn*	-ed ________	-er ________	-ment ________
interest *Ns*	-ed ________	-s ________	-ing ________
introduce *Nds*	-d ________	-s ________	-ing ________
interview *Nvu*	-s ________	-ed ________	-ing ________
establish *esl*	-ed ________	-es ________	-ment ________

WORD CONSTRUCTION

Practice writing these words.

interfere, inter-f-r ________

self-control, self-control ________

intervening, inter-v-n-ing ________

interval, inter-v-l ________

introduction, intro-d-k-tion ________

sampling, sample-ing ________

self-improvement, self-im-prove-ment ________

administrator, administrate-r ________

self-defense, self-d-f-nse ________

controller, control-r ________

WRITING ASSIGNMENT

Self-dictate the following letter as you write it in your shorthand notebook.

Dear Mrs. James:

Your new credit card is enclosed, and we are pleased to welcome you as a charge customer. Your credit[1] limit is shown at the top of this letter.

The attached brochure gives the information you requested about[2] our rose bushes and other plants that would be appropriate for a warm climate. It also refers you to[3] a local dealer to whom you may go for help with your specific landscaping situation. Our dealers are[4] glad to cooperate with our mail-order customers.

You may order either by telephone or by mail,[5] whichever is more convenient. To ensure prompt delivery, we ship by air freight as soon as we receive your[6] order.

If you should have any questions about your new account, please give us a call. Cordially yours, (137)

READING AND WRITING EXERCISES

1

Date

Intro DC

Intro DC

hu r n kl + lv c
rS l s. ul

2

drs evns i rd …
NS u rpl P lq=
lrn gls f clj. … a
i jyn u n Psu s…
v gls u mj-x i Ppz
lae ar . … e …
plnsl brd mbrs,
e … nvi c lcl
S v scls alq …
ppl f bs + N, esd
… e ofn l Dcs
acdc Pgs. ho sl
e idNf c nds vr
knl x … rsrss r
avlB l s x ucd
PbB sug me … gs,
if u agre … ls sa
pln, Intro DC … q … o /

… l. d u p sN
… e . lS v ppl u
plcl … l nvlv x
uvl

3

drs An lqf NS
nr ak fr v dvs
+ dvs. u … o p, Series
ejcyl bcgroN, + Series
acdc aCvms r
v … prsv, edu v .
opn f . Amv asSN.
u jn ofs scls Nca
la udb hil glf f
ls pzj. d ub l Uk
n f . Nvu x ls pzj
cdb . lN Ndcj
lu crr, if u … l
Dcs ls opl frlr, Intro DC
p cl … ofs l ar .
Nvu. lc fw l lc

⌣ u. vlu

4

d⌢rs ⌣i lqf pam
v 40$. ev cr-/ lu
ak, e esp ap u lc
⌢ bl l pln y u
pams vb la. u
ofr l brq ⌢ ak
pda n Jn Snl lb
sal, e lq eno ho
⌢ MUSN dv-ksrn
u upd bN. Ph u
dd n no lau M-
u Ja pam. ⌣n u
sN. dB pam n
Mr, (Intro DC) e apli-/ lu
Ja + Fb nslms. ls
m la uvb l ⌢o
bhN. E pam sN
ln hsb apli- l ⌢
⌢o bf, if ur Sl
pzl-, (Intro DC) p ll s no.
er a NS- n ⌢pv
K Svs. su

5

d⌢r bcr ySrd ih
⌢ plzr v ⌢e. NS
+ hil qlf- aplcN
f. pzj ⌣ r fr. ⌢
dli- lsa la ⌢s
jys yq, no. ⌢pe
n r dla Pss dpl,
iz ⌢prs- b ⌢ rz⌢a
se sN n avN v
Nvu. af ih lc- ⌣
hr n Psn, (Intro DC) i nu /
oN la se db ri f
r ogj. se hs. lN
bcgroN n ofs am,
+ se Ps hrsf z.
cpB + sfasr- ⌢pe,
i ofr- ⌢s yq ⌢ pzj

E kclj v Nvu +
se cl- ls —rn l
ac. er grf lu f rf-

hr l r fr + hp la
fCr Sks l alo s
l rel r fvr. vlu

LESSON 40

1. When a word contains two medial, consecutively pronounced vowels, write the first vowel.

trial, t-r-i-l

annual, an-u-l

premium, pre-m-e-m

previous, pre-v-e-s

various, v-r-e-s

client, k-l-i-nt

material, m-t-r-e-l

actually, a-k-chay-u-l-ly

diagram, d-i-gram

period, p-r-e-d

2. When a word ends in two consecutively pronounced vowel sounds, write only the last vowel.

area, a-r-a

radio, r-d-o

idea, i-d-a

audio, aw-d-o

create, k-r-ate

media, m-d-a

USE A COMMA BEFORE COORDINATE CONJUNCTIONS.

The words *and, or, but, for, nor* are conjunctions. When one of these words connects two complete thoughts, place a comma before it. Make certain that the conjunction is connecting two complete thoughts—that is, either thought can stand alone without the rest of the sentence.

- □ David will type the report, and Susan will distribute it.
- □ I will be gone on Tuesday, but Ms. Hamilton will be glad to help you.
- □ Do you wish to pay for the item now, or shall we charge it to your account?

In your Reading and Writing Exercises, commas before conjunctions will be highlighted with the term **Conj**.

YOUR BUSINESS VOCABULARY

audio-visual ado = vzul

Educational materials (such as filmstrips, movies, video tape programs, and slide/tape programs) that can be seen and heard.

PRINCIPLES SUMMARY

1. When a word contains two medial, consecutively pronounced vowels, write the first vowel: trial, t-r-i-l tril.

2. When a word ends in two consecutively pronounced vowel sounds, write only the last vowel: area, a-r-a ara.

WORD DEVELOPMENT

Write the shorthand outlines for the following related words.

diagram dig	-s ______	-med ______	-ming ______
realize relz	-d ______	-s ______	-ing ______
create cra	-d ______	-s ______	-ing ______
evaluate evla	-s ______	-d ______	-ing ______
graduate grja	-d ______	-s ______	-ing ______

WORD CONSTRUCTION

Practice writing these words.

ideas, i-d-a-s ______	valuation, v-l-u-tion ______
manual, m-n-u-l ______	appliance, a-p-l-i-nce ______
mutual, m-chay-u-l ______	beyond, b-e-nd ______
renewal, re-n-u-l ______	serious, s-r-e-s ______
science, s-i-nce ______	liability, l-i-bil-ity ______

WRITING ASSIGNMENT

Self-dictate the following letter as you write it in your shorthand notebook.

Dear Mr. Harvey:

I want to compliment you on the completion of your new building situated on Park[1] Drive. Our city can be proud of this new addition to our community.

The members of the city council[2] are planning a ribbon-cutting ceremony on the date you requested. The public is invited, and[3] music will be provided by a local high school band. The president of the city council will officially[4] open the ceremony. After he speaks, you will be presented with a key to the city.

Perhaps you have[5] considered conducting tours of the building. While tours are generally not planned, this is no ordinary building.[6] Its special characteristics should be seen to be fully appreciated.

Let us know if we can help[7] make necessary arrangements for the tour. Sincerely, (150)

READING AND WRITING EXERCISES

1

1 p sM me ne lil
uv ab rcrej aras
n u Sa, w pln r
aul fl vcj. er plcl
nS- n htls or aplms
lca- o bC. du uv
brsrs lS rms
avlB n . mdl prs
rnj x, ev Aso hrd
me q lgs ab u Sa
prcs. p sl . cal
dS r prcs, lr fsl ls
(Series) (Series)
& acv ls Pvd- b
eC l, r lr spsl
Sks esd no ab x
r kdjs n u ara
suB f cmp x, ml, r
bze szn fu prcs x,
edb grf f ne Avs
uv lw hlp s pln
. sucf vcj. e lc

fw Uhr f u, su

2

drs an if ur lc
S h crs, u (Intro DC)
spN C vu d
Ppr ls. sdN uv
bl psB trels
Lo x e lq usd.
la, y e cra- r nu
ln v ccr, er so
kvN- v ql' vr
Pdc lae c ls
me=bc grnte. od
u spsl Ndclre sl
+ uz / o . lril bss.
c u dsj E N v
. 30=d pred. if ur
n kpl sal-, u a (Intro DC)
rel / sl. el ln rel
u me, l cs s
so sr ul lv r
ccr x evb f- fn

Pdcs f O 40 yrs, + (Conj)
eno l q ccs lc
f. oN u lri ls plc
sl, ul nvr N luz (Intro DC)
ne els, pv / l usf.
lre usf l s spsl
r cCn. cu

3

dr lr lqf ofr
e / pzj v ado=
vzul drr vu av
ajNe, p- lau
ar . o. , Slnl
njy- e u kvnj
ls o, + s v Ld (Conj)
l ac u ofr. hoE, (Paren)
n n rde l lv
o hr. w bgn
s nu Pgs, + idlc (Conj)
Lc sr la ly r frl
esl- + U kl bf, lv.
sr u USN, ur

lb kq- ou crav o
n rdo + llvq, / db
. Clnj + . plzr Lo
u, chp ls opl
lb psB aq s
n fCr, s

Conj
vluB, + udlc l scyl
v L, Ph / db n
E, s bS NS fe l
hld s lr sys N
v eC pred, lb egr
lhr l u lq, vlu

4

d cl me fn suggs
vb d f r nx ara
sls e, ec pc
lse sv nu fss bcz
v rsN adys n Psnl,
Paren
lrf, blv . rvu vr
bsc Pq db esp hlpf,
/ hs Aso b sug-lae
D sa cpes v A
co lil, sC lil d
Series Series
l cals, sls brsrs,
+ K hNbcs, rcm
la A Psnl alN r
nx ara sls e,
lz e v pv- lb v

5

d elzbl / ajNa f
nx os ara sls
e, no kp, o frS
d . mbr vr sls Sf
l Pvd / Pq rvu u
rqS-, el ln alo /
rS v rn f . q= + =
asr pred, sp Cnys
n S Pdcs lb Dcs-
du / afnn sy, / ls
L / db apo l D
ne nu lil uv re
Series Series
Cnys n prs, Av, or
Dy, / sec d lb
dvo- ntrl l / Py

v nu Pdcs \ r Av_
dpl , Ppr_ (nu
brtrs ⌣ C l Pvd

. u_ adj l r S_ lil >
idb grf f ne sugjs
u ⌢a v \ cu

LESSON 41

1. Write T for the word beginnings *tran* and *trans*.

transfer, trans-f-r Tfr

transcribe, tran-scribe TS

tranquil, tran-q-l Tql

transistor, trans-st-r TSr

translate, trans-l-ate Tla

transportation, trans-port-tion Tpj

2. Always use the word beginnings *trans, sur,* and *com* for blending sounds.

transact, trans-a-k Tac

surround, sur-ow-nd SoN

community, com-n-ity kn[l]

Otherwise, avoid blending the initial sound of a major accented syllable with a preceding syllable.

indulge, in-d-l-j ndlj

entire, en-t-r ntr

addition, a-d-tion adj

allow, a-l-ow alo

WRITING UNUSUAL WORDS

Those proper nouns, technical terms, or unusual words that might be misspelled or transcribed incorrectly can be written in full. In addition, abbreviations or writing shortcuts familiar to the shorthand writer can be used in recording notes. The following sentence is an example.

Mr. Aillet is head of the word processing department at Yazoo Industries.

—r aillet , hd v wp dpl / Yazoo Ns.

USE COMMAS WITH INTRODUCTORY PHRASES.

An introductory infinitive phrase (a verb preceded by *to*) is followed by a comma.

□ To get our proposal completed, we had to work for three months after closing hours.

An introductory participial phrase (a verb form used as an adjective) is followed by a comma.

□ Leaving her umbrella at the office, the secretary got wet while running to catch her bus.

An introductory prepositional phrase or phrases consisting of five or more words, or an introductory prepositional phrase containing a verb form is followed by a comma.

□ In two or three days, I will be finished with the inventory.
□ At the beginning of our employment with Brown and Company, we were required to complete a training course.
□ After giving considerable thought to your suggestion, we have decided to adopt the proposal.

In the Reading and Writing Exercises, the abbreviation **Intro P** will be used to highlight introductory phrases.

YOUR BUSINESS VOCABULARY

transaction *Tac* The completion or carrying out of an exchange of things of value, frequently preceded by negotiation.

premiums *Prms* In reference to insurance, the payments on an insurance policy.

PRINCIPLES SUMMARY

1. Write *T* for the word beginnings *tran* and *trans*: transfer, trans-f-r *Tfr*

2. Always use the word beginnings *trans, sur,* and *com* for blending sounds; otherwise, avoid blending the initial sound of a major accented syllable with a preceding syllable.

WORD CONSTRUCTION

Write the shorthand outlines for the following related words.

act *ac*	-ed ________	-ing ________	trans- ________
plant *pln*	-s ________	-ed ________	trans- ________
late *la*	re- ________	-ly ________	trans- ________
form *f*	re- ________	con- ________	trans- ________
port *pl*	im- ________	ex- ________	trans- ________

WORD DEVELOPMENT

Practice writing these words.

transmit, trans-m-t ________

tranquilize, tran-q-l-z ________

transforming, trans-for-m-ing ________

transistors, trans-st-r-s ________

transcript, tran-script ________

transpose, trans-p-z ________

transferred, trans-f-r-duh ________

tranquility, tran-q-l-ity ________

transaction, trans-a-k-tion ________

transmission, trans-m-sion ________

WRITING ASSIGNMENT

Self-dictate the following letter as you write it in your shorthand notebook.

Dear Mrs. Lee:

In the event of an accident involving someone in your family, you would want help to[1] arrive immediately. Our city is in need of new emergency equipment, and we are asking you[2] to contribute to our fund drive.

We want our equipment to correspond to the standards characteristic of[3] other cities the size of ours. With increased demands for the use of our tax dollars, money for new equipment[4] is just not available. We think we can overcome this difficult situation by gaining the support[5] of concerned citizens like you in our various neighborhoods.

Our current goal is to raise enough money for[6] one new ambulance. Won't you send us a donation in the enlcosed envelope? Then you, too, will help in fulfilling[7] a vital need in our community. Sincerely yours, (151)

READING AND WRITING EXERCISES

1

Intro P

Series Series Series

Date

Paren

Intro P

2

kgjs f c ls yrs fM drv / bgs + bs E, e rC- r gl 2 cs ahd v L. n / drv N- o Oc 4, (Intro DC) eh vd- A pcjs, l ls r no trel rws aso- vlnls o, (Intro DC) eno u sr r fl v aCvm + saly. e s l lq E, hu hlp- n Ppr rdo + nzppr Avms, (Series) n Pvd Tply, (Series) + n c Hs v cls, u hlp- c ls drv. suc, (Conj) + er grf lu f pl u Bls o f s. uvl

e agre- po. p nl S alC- dig la / nu prp ln hsb clrl dfn-. / c no lgr b kfz- SoN aras. cpes v ls rvq dl- l / nu ors ySrd, (Conj) + ly gv / ls apvl, af A u sig l A 3 cpes v kc, (Intro P) ul nd l rel l e. oN uv sn- / fs, (Intro DC) / kc bks fnl. / Ul lu prp, ln Tfr- l / nu ors, uv kgjs o hNl ls ls sol. Tay sC z ls ordl lcs sv cs. ls hsb rzlv- qcl + kvl bcz v hlp v E, nvlv-, chp ul

3

ds evns / enc- rl eSa kc hsb rvz- l e / ls

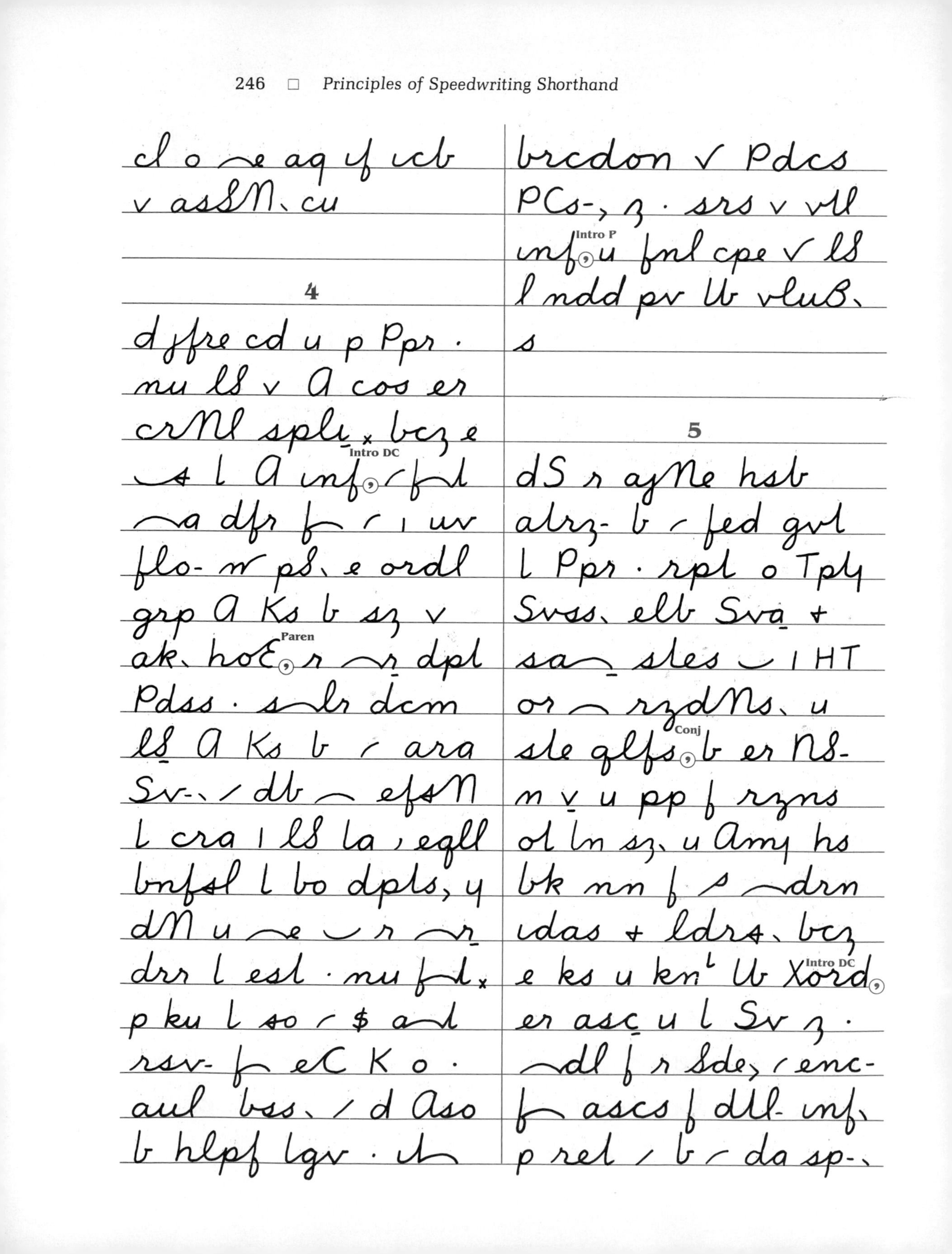

Intro P

4

Intro DC

Paren

5

Conj

Intro DC

cd u Aso spli s ⌣
lil ou Tply cos.
edlc lno ab
scjls, (Series) frs, (Series) +
No v cliNs uz-

r Svss o . dl
bss, zz r rzlts
vb pbls-, (Intro DC) el ~l
Nv cpes l A pp-
sles. su

LESSON 42

RECAP AND REVIEW

1. You learned to write the following word beginnings in Lessons 36–41:

sub s

tran, trans T

enter, inter, intro N

self sf

2. You also learned these word endings:

ful f

self sf

ify f

selves svs

ification fl

3. Write these words that illustrate all of the new principles you studied in Lessons 36–41:

effective, e-f-k-tive efcv

himself, him-self hsf

grateful, grate-ful grf

ourselves, our-selves rsvs

qualify, q-l-ify qlf

trial, t-r-i-l tril

qualification, q-l-ification qlfl

idea, i-d-a ida

interview, inter-v-u Nvu

transcribe, tran-scribe TS

self-addressed, self-a-d-r-s-duh sfadrs-

since, s-nce sN

4. Transcribe the following abbreviations:

esl

S

5. How quickly can you write these brief forms?

usual __________	once __________	work __________
circumstance __________	manufacture __________	administrate __________
world __________	significance __________	signature __________
significant __________	particular __________	sample __________
control __________		

READING AND WRITING EXERCISES

1

ds jcsn r rqS
f fNs hsb apv-.
l Sv r sle + SoN
Intro P
ara, ec no esl
r Ppz- ldrs Pq.
sr u USN c ssl
sig v ls Pq. cliNs
Czn l pp lb lrn-
n ldrs lds.
oN c cliNs v
Intro DC
kp- r crs, ly lb
ncrj- l dr ol
ls Pgs n r knl,
r objcv no, l
lca . vp- Psn l ld
r lrn sjs. eblv
u lb c S glf- Psn
bcz vu aCvms n
vlnlr o. d ub
l l Sv z Px, v
Paren
crs, ul s lgv
ls lr crf ksf.p
alo e l asr ne
qs u a v / ls
. s

2

dr — lsn u
ano Nm k z — Nrf
nz. sC. Pq, Sln
Ub sucf n ls kn'.
dd i USN crcl la
. grN hsb aw- f ls
Pjc., grN sf, gi
. akm. kgjs q lu +
ol Nvs hu s-d-
Ppzl, idb hpe l
Sv ou brd v drrs, (Conj)
b icn ac pzj v
P. Amv dles d
rq — ln — P
Sks alo. hoE, ic (Paren)
lq v sv ppl hu v
—d siq kbjs n
vlntr —o. d u
lc —e l rcm loz
hu — b NS- n bk
P., ifl p- Ub ks- f
ls pzj. lqf vo v
kfdN. cu

3

d ble. fu —cs aq
u prs- NS n —o
f r co. / la — eh
no opn lofr u.
sN Sks v Cnj-, ic (Intro DC)
no rf u l. pzj
—C bk avlS ol
ySrd, — enc. jb
dS f ofs v Amv
sec. a aplcNs
—S v Pves p n
ofs —o + scl n
srlhN l qlf f ls
pzj. zi rcl, uv (Intro DC)
Ar est-. —prsv
bcgroN —C ds
ri + TS srlhN
PfsNl, if u —s l
apli, p cl — ofs (Intro DC)
b Fr afnn. ec ln

ar . Nvu l Dcs (
pzy frls. uvl

4

d-r rbrls uv . q
re r uz Psyr f pa
ins cls f -dcl
vzls, e ordl avz (
-pe l P (f- f
drs sig dy (vzl.
Paren
n s- css, (dr
rqSs adyl l- f N
inf rlv l la vzl.
(f- , ln -l- l (
Conj
-pe, + -pe s-ls
(l r ofs, ls Psyr
as sv ds bln (l-
(-pe pas f vzl +
da (f- arvs n r
Intro DC
ofs. oN (f-s k n,
e Pss l- -l + usu
. Cc l (-pe. b la
Paren Paren
l-, hoE, (lol Tacy

hs lcn p l 3 -cs,
lr -S b . -a l sv
Pss l-. idb grf
fu idas o ls syc. ul

5

mo l A -pes p-la
crlsn l bk jn -yr
vr -f. dvy z v Jl 1,
Intro DC
-n (Cny bks efcv,
(-f. dvy lb pN-l
I 2 nu dpls. (ofs
v Nl rSC lb rspB
Conj
f lq=rny pln, + .
sS-s kl dpl l nsr
ku- lN f r Pdc. ulb
hr - ab bo v lz
dvms n nr fCr,
v jyn- r Sf z
Intro P
. nynr, p-la brl
me fn idas l r opy.
se hs ac- z S f
Conj
spsl Pjcs, + -S

rsNl se hs Sv- z
ad alS n r Nnyl
dvj, n sr p-la
l lk u asSN n gl

esl- n hr nu ofs.
se , lc fur Lo
eC vu.

BRIEF FORMS BY ORDER OF PRESENTATION

The numeral in the upper left corner of a box indicates the lesson in which the brief forms were introduced. To use the table as a reference for brief forms in the order of their presentation, read from left to right across each numbered row.

	A	B	C	D	E	F	G	H
1	1 .	/	)	m	r	l	e	l
2	2 r	c	b	v	s	4 fr	fr	L
3	⌒y	⌒r	ȯ	pl	Ph	d	u	6 ac
4	af	apo	b	dl	du	nes	y	9 ar
5	z	jn	gr	hsp	la	⌣	11 bln	op
6	pp	py	prp	rf	rsp	s	sil	sug
7	loz	13 ⌒	G	dr	q	h	ly	16 ap
8	cor	D	p	P	sp	18 ab	K	hs
9	‿l	od	O	U	20 avj	aq	bs	sv
10	22 crc	E	N	ol	sal	24 ak	k	kp
11	ku	kb	kv	dl	opl	26 bo	‿pl	Nv
12	pb	27 a	ks	nl	ord	pv	30 Ar	apx
13	vp	⌒	nx	32 B	kc	dfc	‿p	opn
14	34 acq	aso	kq	dv	oq	Sd	suc	37 ‿f
15	siq	uz	‿o	39 Am	Sk	kl	oN	pkc
16	sa‿							

ABBREVIATIONS BY ORDER OF PRESENTATION

The numeral in the upper left corner of a box indicates the lesson in which the abbreviations were introduced. To use the table as a reference for abbreviations in the order of their presentation, read from left to right across each numbered row.

	A	B	C	D	E	F	G	H
1	2 +	cal	co	inf	p	rel	VP	4 m
2	~r	~rs	~s	6 corp	E	enc	N	S
3	W	9 a~l	all	cr	No	%	lol	11 dpl
4	env	ins	inv	re	13 jr	sec	sr	16 ave
5	blvd	d	ex	hr	~o	rec	18 B	¢
6	$	H	in	M	oz	lb	T	20 agr
7	eco	ft	sq	yd	22 esp	etc	~dse	gl
8	q	U	24 fed	gvt	inc	ok	rep	S
9	27 av	X~s	34 a~	ltd	vol	39 est	S	

PHRASES BY ORDER OF PRESENTATION

The numeral in the upper left corner of a box indicates the lesson in which the phrases were introduced. To use the table as a reference for phrases in the order of their presentation, read from left to right across each numbered row.

	A	B	C	D	E	F	G	H
1	13 [illegible]	ic	ch	cv	il	ilb	er	ec
2	ev	ehp	ed	edb	ur	uc	uv	uno
3	ul	ud	lb	lq	lv	lvu	lvu	lno
4	lpa	lqf	lqf	lqfL	15 cd	chp	lse	f
5	v	lau	lau	lb	db	s	16 cd	cdap
6	cdb	esd	el	edap	ucb	udlc	[illegible]	[illegible]
7	lae	17 cblv	udu	usd	lcp	cdb	fu	fu
8	nr	vu	vu	lu	lu	18 edu	efl	und
9	[illegible]c	vb	vr	lu	lu	19 eap	eh	e[illegible]
10	u[illegible]	luz	vh	6	20 cno	ern	elb	ulb
11	lgl	lhr	lsn	cb	22 cvb	csd	cz	eblv
12	eno	zlz	23 cdlc	erp-	ucn	ucd	lrsv	lsa
13	24 cfl	udb	zz	ze	25 lc	ecd	evb	edlc
14	ldu	lgv	lvzl	26 lk	lofr	ldl	29 ulfn	lcl
15	zu	zu	ou	ou	31 zi	hsb	sdb	lqu
16	dlc	33 nvrls	nnls	[illegible]	pda	36 laur	laul	37 cap
17	lo	lai	appendix ccb	ccn	cdu	cvh	csl	ecb
18	ecn	evh	esl	uh	uvb	uvh	zl	fcla
19	vn	vu	vu					

KEY TO BRIEF FORMS

	A	B	C	D	E	F	G	H
1	1 a an	it at	is his	in not	the	to too	we	will well
2	2 are our	can	for full	of have very	us	4 firm	from	letter
3	manage	market	on own	part port	perhaps	would	your	6 accept
4	after	appropriate	be, but, been buy, by	determine	during	necessary	why	9 arrange
5	as was	general	great grate	hospital	that	were with	11 between	operate
6	participate	point	property	refer	respond response	ship	situate	suggest
7	those	13 am more	charge	doctor direct	go good	he had him	they	16 appreciate
8	correspond correspon- dence	distribute	please up	present	specific specify	18 about	customer	has
9	include	order	over	under	20 advantage	again against	business	several
10	22 character characteristic	ever every	industry	other	satisfy satisfactory	24 accomplish	come came committee	complete
11	continue	contribute	convenient convenience	deliver	opportunity	26 both	important importance	individual
12	public	27 always	consider	note	ordinary	prove	30 already	approximate
13	experience	immediate	next	32 able	contract	difficult	employ	opinion
14	34 acknowledge	associate	congratulate	develop	organize	standard	success	37 manufacture
15	signature significant significance	usual	work world	39 administrate	circumstance	control	once	particular
16	sample							

KEY TO ABBREVIATIONS

	A	B	C	D	E	F	G	H
1	**2** and	catalog	company	information	president	return	vice president	**4** Miss
2	Mr.	Mrs.	Ms.	**6** corporation	east	enclose enclosure	north	south
3	west	**9** amount	attention	credit	number	percent	total	**11** department
4	envelope	insurance	invoice	regard	**13** junior	second secretary	senior	**16** avenue
5	boulevard	day	example executive	hour	month	record	**18** billion	cent cents
6	dollar dollars	hundred	inch	million	ounce	pound	thousand	**20** agriculture
7	economic economy	feet	square	yard	**22** especially	et cetera	merchandise	quart
8	question	university	**24** federal	government	incorporate incorporated	okay	represent representative	street
9	**27** advertise	Christmas	**34** America American	literature	volume	**39** establish	superintendent	

KEY TO PHRASES

	A	B	C	D	E	F	G	H
1	13 I am	I can	I had	I have	I will	I will be	we are	we can
2	we have	we hope	we would	we would be	you are	you can	you have	you know
3	you will	you would	to be	to go	to have	to have you	to have your	to know
4	to pay	thank you for	thank you for your	thank you for your letter	15 I could	I hope	to see	for the
5	of the	that you	that your	will be	would be	it is	16 I would	I would appreciate
6	I would be	we should	we will	we would appreciate	you can be	you would like	and the	at the
7	that we	17 I believe	you do	you should	to keep	could be	for you	for your
8	in the	of you	of your	will you	will your	18 we do	we feel	you need
9	to make	have been	of our	to you	to your	19 we appreciate	we had	we were
10	you were	to use	have had	on the	20 I know	we are not	we will be	you will be
11	to get	to hear	to send	can be	22 I have been	I should	I was	we believe
12	we know	as well as	23 I would like	we are pleased	you cannot	you could	to receive	to say
13	24 I feel	you would be	as soon as	as we	25 I look	we could	we have been	we would like
14	to do	to give	to visit	26 to come	to offer	to determine	29 you will find	to call
15	as you	as your	on you	on your	31 as I	has been	should be	thank you
16	would like	33 nevertheless	nonetheless	time to time	up to date	36 that you are	that you will	37 I appreciate
17	to work	that I	**appendix** I can be	I cannot	I do	I have had	I shall	we can be
18	we cannot	we have had	we shall	you had	you have been	you have had	as to	fact that
19	have not	have you	have your					

BRIEF FORMS BY ALPHABETICAL ORDER

Word	Brief form
a (an)	·
able	B
about	ab
accept	ac
accomplish	ak
acknowledge	acj
administrate	am
advantage	avj
after	af
again (against)	aq
against (again)	aq
already	ar
always	a
am (more)	⌒
an (a)	·
appreciate	ap
appropriate	apo
approximate	apx
are (our)	r
arrange	ar
as (was)	z
associate	aso
at (it)	/
be (been, but, buy, by)	b
been (be, but, buy, by)	b
between	btn
both	bo
business	bs
but (be, been, buy, by)	b
buy (be, been, but, by)	b
by (be, been, but, buy)	b
came (come, committee)	k
can	c
character (characteristic)	crc
characteristic (character)	crc
charge	Cj
circumstance	Sk
come (came, committee)	k
committee (came, come)	k
complete	kp
congratulate	kq
consider	ks

continue ku
contract kc
contribute kb
control kl
convenience (convenient) kv
convenient (convenience) kv
correspond (correspondence) cor
correspondence (correspond) cor
customer K
deliver dl
determine dl
develop dv
difficult dfc
direct (doctor) dr
distribute D
doctor (direct) dr
during du
employ [curve]p
ever (every) E
every (ever) E
experience vp
firm fr
for (full) f
from f
full (for) f
general jn
go (good) g
good (go) g
grate (great) gr
great (grate) gr
had (he, him) h
has hs
have (of, very) v
he (had, him) h
him (had, he) h
his (is))
hospital hsp
immediate [curve]
importance (important) [curve]pl
important (importance) [curve]pl
in (not) n
include [curve]l
individual Nv
industry N
is (his))
it (at) /

letter

manage

manufacture

market

more (am)

necessary

next

not (in)

note

of (have, very)

on (own)

once

operate

opinion

opportunity

order

ordinary

organize

other

our (are)

over

own (on)

part (port)

participate

particular

perhaps

please (up)

point

port (part)

present

property

prove

public

refer

respond (response)

response (respond)

sample

satisfactory (satisfy)

satisfy (satisfactory)

several

ship

signature (significance, significant)

significance (signature, significant)

significant (signature, significance)

situate sit

specific (specify) sp

specify (specific) sp

standard Sd

success suc

suggest sug

that Ta

the

they Ty

those Toz

to (too) T

too (to) T

under U

up (please) p

us s

usual uz

very (have, of) v

was (as) z

we e

well (will) l

were (with)

why y

will (well) l

with (were)

work (world)

world (work)

would d

your u

ABBREVIATIONS BY ALPHABETICAL ORDER

advertise av
agriculture agr
America (American) am
American (America) am
amount amt
and +
attention att
avenue ave
billion B
boulevard blvd
catalog cat
cent (cents) ¢
cents (cent) ¢
Christmas Xmas
company co
corporation corp
credit cr
day d
department dpt
dollar (dollars) $
dollars (dollar) $

east E
economic (economy) eco
economy (economic) eco
enclose (enclosure) enc
enclosure (enclose) enc
envelope env
especially esp
establish est
et cetera etc
example (executive) ex
executive (example) ex
federal fed
feet ft
government gvt
hour hr
hundred H
inch in
incorporate (incorporated) inc
incorporated (incorporate) inc
information inf
insurance ins

invoice inv

junior jr

literature lit

merchandise mdse

million M

Miss M

month mo

Mr. mr

Mrs. mrs

Ms. ms

north N

number No

okay ok

ounce oz

percent %

pound lb

president P

quart qt

question q

record rec

regard re

represent (representative) rep

representative (represent) rep

return ret

second (secretary) sec

secretary (second) sec

senior sr

south S

square sq

street S

superintendent S

thousand T

total tot

university U

vice president VP

volume vol

west W

yard yd

PHRASES BY ORDER OF CATEGORY

The following phrases are presented in alphabetical segments beginning with the pronouns *I, we,* and *you* plus a verb, followed by infinitive phrases (*to* plus a verb), high-frequency word combinations, and word combinations with words omitted.

I am

I appreciate

I believe

I can

I can be

I cannot

I could

I do

I feel

I had

I have

I have been

I have had

I hope

I know

I look

I shall

I should

I was

I will

I will be

I would

I would appreciate

I would be

I would like

we appreciate

we are

we are not

we are pleased

we believe

we can

we can be

we cannot

we could

we do

we feel

we had

we have

we have been evb
we have had evh
we hope ehp
we know eno
we shall esl
we should esd
we were e—
we will el
we will be elb
we would ed
we would appreciate edap
we would be edb
we would like edlc
you are ur
you can uc
you cannot ucn
you can be ucb
you could ucd
you do udu
you had uh
you have uv
you have been uvb
you have had uvh

you know uno
you need und
you should usd
you were u—
you will ul
you will be ulb
you will find ulfN
you would ud
you would be udb
you would like udlc
to be lb
to call lcl
to come lk
to determine ldl
to do ldu
to get lgl
to give lgv
to go lq
to have lv
to have you lvu
to have your lvu
to hear lhr
to keep lcp

to know

to make

to offer

to pay

to receive

to say

to see

to send

to use

to visit

to work

and the

as I

as to

as we

as well as

as you

as your

at the

can be

could be

fact that

for the

for you

for your

has been

have been

have had

have not

have you

have your

in the

it is

of our

of the

of you

of your

on the

on you

on your

should be

thank you

that I

that we

that you

that you are

that you will laul
that your lau
to you lu
to your lu
will be lb
will you lu
will your lu
would be db
would like dlc

as soon as zz
nevertheless nvrls
nonetheless nnls
thank you for lqf
thank you for your lqf
thank you for your letter lqfL
time to time t-t
up to date pda

IDENTIFICATION INITIALS FOR UNITED STATES AND TERRITORIES

Alabama (AL) AL

Alaska (AK) AK

Arizona (AZ) AZ

Arkansas (AR) AR

California (CA) CA

Colorado (CO) CO

Connecticut (CT) CT

Delaware (DE) DE

District of Columbia (DC) DC

Florida (FL) FL

Georgia (GA) GA

Hawaii (HI) HI

Idaho (ID) ID

Illinois (IL) IL

Indiana (IN) IN

Iowa (IA) IA

Kansas (KS) KS

Kentucky (KY) KY

Louisiana (LA) LA

Maine (ME) ME

Maryland (MD) MD

Massachusetts (MA) MA

Michigan (MI) MI

Minnesota (MN) MN

Mississippi (MS) MS

Missouri (MO) MO

Montana (MT) MT

Nebraska (NE) NE

Nevada (NV) NV

New Hampshire (NH) NH

New Jersey (NJ) NJ

New Mexico (NM) NM

New York (NY) NY

North Carolina (NC) NC

North Dakota (ND) ND

Ohio (OH) OH

Oklahoma (OK) OK

Oregon (OR) OR

Pennsylvania (PA) PA

Rhode Island (RI) RI

South Carolina (SC) SC

South Dakota (SD) SD

Tennessee (TN) TN

Texas (TX) TX

Utah (UT) UT

Vermont (VT) VT

Virginia (VA) VA

Washington (WA) WA

West Virginia (WV) WV

Wisconsin (WI) WI

Wyoming (WY) WY

Canal Zone (CZ) CZ

Guam (GU) GU

Puerto Rico (PR) PR

Virgin Islands (VI) VI

CANADIAN PROVINCES AND TERRITORIES

Alberta (AB) AB

British Columbia (BC) BC

Labrador (LB) LB

Manitoba (MB) MB

New Brunswick (NB) NB

Newfoundland (NF) NF

Northwest Territories (NT) NT

Nova Scotia (NS) NS

Ontario (ON) ON

Prince Edward Island (PE) PE

Quebec (PQ) PQ

Saskatchewan (SK) SK

Yukon Territory (YT) YT

METRIC TERMS

	meter (length) m	liter (capacity) l	gram (weight) g
kilo	km	kl	kg
hecto	hm	hl	hg
deca	dam	dal	dag
deci	dm	dl	dg
centi	cm	cl	cg
milli	mm	ml	mg
micro	mcrm	mcrl	mcrg
nano	nm	nl	ng

SPEEDWRITING SHORTHAND PRINCIPLES BY ORDER OF PRESENTATION

Principle	Word	Outline	Word	Outline
1. Write what you hear.	high	hi		
2. Drop medial vowels.	build	bld		
3. Write initial and final vowels.	office	ofs	fee	fe
4. Write c for the sound of *k*.	copy	cpe		
5. Write a capital C for the sound of *ch*.	check	Cc		
6. Write ⌒ for the sound of *m*.	may	⌒a		
7. Write ‿ for the sound of *w* and *wh*.	way	‿a	when	‿n
8. Underscore the last letter of any outline to add *ing* or *thing* as a word ending.	billing	bl_	something	s⌒_
9. To form the plural of any outline ending in a mark of punctuation, double the last mark of punctuation.	savings	sv=		
10. Write s to form the plural of any outline, to show possession, or to add s to a verb.	books	bcs	runs	rns
11. Write m for the sounds of *mem* and *mum*.	memo	mo		
12. Write m for the sounds of *men, min, mon, mun*.	menu	mu	money	me
13. Write m for the word endings *mand, mend, mind, ment*.	demand	dm	amend	am
	remind	rm	payment	pam
14. Write a capital N for the sound of *nt*.	sent	sN		

15. Write *ɟ* for the sound of *ish* or *sh*.	finish	*fnɟ*		
16. Write a capital *a* for the word beginnings *ad, all, al.*	admit	*a-*	also	*aso*
17. Write *m* for the initial sound of *in* or *en*.	indent	*ndN*		
18. Write *o* for the sound of *ow*.	allow	*alo*		
19. Write a printed capital *S* (joined) for the word beginnings *cer, cir, ser, sur.*	certain	*Sln*	survey	*Sva*
20. To form the past tense of a regular verb, write a hyphen after the outline.	used	*uz-*		
21. Write *l* for the sound of *ith* or *th*.	them	*lm*		
22. Write *l* for the word ending *ly* or *ily*.	family	*fl*		
23. Write a capital *D* for the word beginning *dis*.	discuss	*Dcs*		
24. Write a capital *M* for the word beginning *mis*.	misplace	*Mpls*		
25. Retain beginning or ending vowels when building compound words.	payroll	*parl*	headache	*hdac*
26. Retain root-word vowels when adding prefixes and suffixes.	disappear	*Dapr*	payment	*pam*
27. Write a capital *P* (disjoined) for the word beginnings *per, pur, pre, pro, pro* (prah).	person	*Psn*	prepare	*Ppr*
	provide	*Pvd*	problem	*Pbl*
28. Write *g* for the word ending *gram*.	telegram	*tlg*		

Rule		Example		Example	
29. Write y for the sound of *oi.*		boy	by		
30. For words ending in a long vowel + *t*, omit the *t* and write the vowel.		rate	ra	meet	me
31. Write a for the word beginning *an.*		answer	asr		
32. Write q for the medial or final sound of any vowel + *nk.*		bank	bq	link	lq
33. Write a capital S (disjoined) for the word beginning *super* and for the word endings *scribe* and *script.*		supervise	S vz	describe	dS
		manuscript	mnS		
34. Write el for the word beginning *electr.*		electronic	elnc		
35. Write w for the word ending *ward.*		backward	bcw		
36. Write h for the word ending *hood.*		boyhood	byh		
37. Write 1 for the word ending *tion* or *sion.*		vacation	vc1		
38. Write a for the initial and final sound of *aw.*		law	la	audit	adt
39. Write q for the sound of *kw.*		quick	qc		
40. Write a capital N for the sound of *nd.*		friend	frN		
41. Write ⌒ for the initial sound of *em* or *im.*		emphasize	⌒fsz	impress	⌒prs
42. Omit *p* in the sound of *mpt.*		prompt	P⌒t		

Principle	Word	Shorthand	Word	Shorthand
43. Write k for the sounds of *com, con, coun, count.*	common	kn	convey	kva
	counsel	ksl	account	ak
44. Write 8 for the sound of *st.*	rest	r8		
45. Write q for the word ending *quire.*	require	rq		
46. Write 3 for the sound of zh.	pleasure	plzr		
47. Write ′ for the word ending *ness.*	kindness	cN′		
48. Write \ for words beginning with the sound of any vowel + x.	explain	\pln	accident	\dN
49. Write x for the medial and final sound of x.	boxes	bxs	relax	rlx
50. Write X for the word beginnings *extr* and *extra.*	extreme	X—		
	extraordinary	Xord		
51. Write q for the medial or final sound of any vowel + *ng.*	rang	rq	single	sgl
52. Write B for the word endings *bil, ble, bly.*	possible	psB	probably	PbB
53. Omit the final *t* of a root word after the sound of *k.*	act	ac		
54. Write ˡ (slightly raised and disjoined) for the word ending *ity.*	quality	qlˡ		
55. Write u for the word beginning *un.*	until	ull		

Rule	Word	Shorthand
56. Write sl for the sound of *shul* and for the word ending *chul.*	financial	fnnsl
57. Write N for the sounds of *ance, ence, nce, nse.*	expense	xpN
58. Write s for the word beginning *sub.*	submit	smt
59. Write v for the medial and final sound of *tive.*	effective	efcv
60. Write f for the word endings *ful* and *ify.*	careful	crf
	justify	jsf
61. Write fj for the word ending *ification*	qualifications	qlfjs
62. Write a capital N for the word beginnings *enter, inter, intro.*	enterprise	Nprz
	introduce	Nds
	interest	Ns
63. Write sf for the word beginning and ending *self.*	self-made	sfmd
	myself	msf
64. Write svs for the word ending *selves.*	ourselves	rsvs
65. When a word contains two medial, consecutively pronounced vowels, write the first vowel.	trial	tril
66. When a word ends in two consecutively pronounced vowels, write only the last vowel.	idea	ida
67. Write T for the word beginnings *tran* and *trans.*	transfer	Tfr

SPEEDWRITING SHORTHAND PRINCIPLES BY SYSTEM CATEGORY

Simple Sounds

Principle	Word	Outline	Lesson
1. Write what you hear.	high	hi	1
2. Write c for the sound of *k*.	copy	cpe	2
3. Write for the sound of *m*.	may		2
4. Write for the sound of *w*.	way		2
5. Write s to form the plural of any outline, to show possession, or to add s to a verb.	books	bcs	
	runs	rns	2
6. Omit *p* in the sound of *mpt*.	empty		22
7. Write x for the medial and final sound of x.	boxes	bxs	
	tax	tx	29
8. Omit the final *t* of a root word after the sound of *k*.	act	ac	31

Vowels

Principle	Word	Outline	Lesson
1. Drop medial vowels.	build	bld	1
2. Write initial and final vowels.	office	ofs	
	fee	fe	1
3. Retain beginning or ending vowels when building compound words.	payroll	parl	
	headache	hdac	9
4. Retain root-word vowels when adding prefixes and suffixes.	disappear	Dapr	
	payment	pam	9

Rule	Example	Shorthand	Lesson
5. For words ending in a long vowel + *t*, omit the *t* and write the vowel.	rate	ra	
	meet	⌒e	12
6. When a word contains two medial, consecutively pronounced vowels, write the first vowel.	trial	tril	40
7. When a word ends in two consecutively pronounced vowels, write only the last vowel.	idea	ida	40

Vowel Blends

Rule	Example	Shorthand	Lesson
1. Write o for the sound of *ow*.	allow	alo	5
2. Write y for the sound of *oi*.	boy	by	11
3. Write a for the initial and final sound of *aw*.	law	la	
	audit	adl	19

Consonant Blends

Rule	Example	Shorthand	Lesson
1. Write a capital C for the sound of *ch*.	check	Cc	2
2. Write ⌣ for the sound of *wh*.	when	⌣n	2
3. Write a capital N for the sound of *nt*.	sent	sN	3
4. Write ɇ for the sound of *ish* or *sh*.	finish	fnɇ	4
5. Write l for the sound of *ith* or *th*.	them	l⌒	8
6. Write q for the medial or final sound of any vowel + *nk*.	bank	bq	
	link	lq	13

7. Write q for the sound of *kw*.	quick	qc	19
8. Write a capital N for the sound of *nd*.	friend	frN	20
9. Write 8 for the sound of *st*.	rest	r8	23
10. Write z for the sound of *zh*.	pleasure	plzr	25
11. Write g for the medial or final sound of any vowel + *ng*.	rang	rg	
	single	sgl	30
12. Write M for the sounds of *ance, ence, nce, nse*.	balance	blM	36

Compound Sounds

1. Write m for the sounds of *mem* and *mum*.	memo	mo	3
2. Write m for the sounds of *men, min, mon, mun*.	menu	mu	
	money	me	3
3. Write k for the sounds of *com, con, coun, count*.	common	kn	
	convey	kva	
	counsel	ksl	
	account	ak	23

Word Beginnings

1. Write a capital A for the word beginnings *ad, all,* and *al*.	admit	Ad	
	also	Aso	4

Principle	Word	Outline	Page
2. Write *n* for the initial sound of *in* and *en*.	indent	ndN	4
3. Write a printed capital S (joined) for the word beginnings *cer, cir, ser, sur*.	certain	Sln	
	survey	Sva	5
4. Write a capital D for the word beginning *dis*.	discuss	Dcs	8
5. Write a capital M for the word beginning *mis*.	misplace	Mpls	8
6. Write a capital P (disjoined) for the word beginnings *per, pur, pre, pro, pro* (prah).	person	Psn	
	prepare	Ppr	
	provide	Pvd	
	problem	Pbl	10
7. Write *a* for the word beginning *an*.	answer	asr	13
8. Write a capital S (disjoined) for the word beginning *super*.	supervise	Svz	15
9. Write *el* for the word beginning *electr*.	electronic	elnc	15
10. Write ⌒ for the initial sound of *em* or *im*.	emphasize	⌒fsz	
	impress	⌒prs	22
11. Write \ for words beginning with the sound of any vowel + x.	explain	\pln	
	accident	\dN	29
12. Write X for the word beginnings *extr* and *extra*.	extreme	X⌒	
	extraordinary	Xord	29
13. Write *u* for the word beginning *un*.	until	ull	33

Principle	Example	Page
14. Write s for the word beginning *sub.*	submit	36
15. Write a capital N for the word beginnings *enter, inter, intro.*	enterprise	
	interest	
	introduce	39
16. Write sf for the word beginning *self.*	self-made	39
17. Write T for the word beginnings *tran* and *trans.*	transfer	41

Word Endings

Principle	Example	Page
1. Underscore the last letter of the outline to add *ing* or *thing* as a word ending.	billing	
	something	2
2. To form the plural of any outline ending in a mark of punctuation, double the last mark of punctuation.	savings	2
3. To form the past tense of a regular verb, write a hyphen after the outline.	used	6
4. Write m for the word endings *mand, mend, mind, ment.*	demand	
	amend	
	remind	
	payment	3
5. Write l for the word ending *ly* or *ily.*	family	8
6. Write g for the word ending *gram.*	telegram	10

Rule	Word	Shorthand	Page
7. Write a capital S (disjoined) for the word endings *scribe* and *script*.	describe	dS	
	manuscript	mnS	15
8. Write w for the word ending *ward*.	backward	bcw	16
9. Write h for the word ending *hood*.	boyhood	byh	16
10. Write j for the word ending *tion* or *sion*.	vacation	vcj	17
11. Write q for the word ending *quire*.	require	rq	25
12. Write ' for the word ending *ness*.	kindness	cN'	26
13. Write B for the word endings *bil, ble, bly*.	possible	psB	
	probably	PbB	31
14. Write c (slightly raised and disjoined) for the word ending *ity*.	quality	ql^c	32
15. Write sl for the sound of *shul* and the word ending *chul*.	financial	fnnsl	34
16. Write v for the medial and final sound of *tive*.	effective	efcv	37
17. Write f for the word endings *ful* and *ify*.	careful	crf	
	justify	jsf	38
18. Write fj for the word ending *ification*.	qualifications	qlfjs	38
19. Write sf for the word ending *self*.	myself	-sf	39
20. Write svs for the word ending *selves*.	ourselves	rsvs	39

Marks of Punctuation

1. Underscore the last letter of the outline to add *ing* or *thing* as a word ending. billing, something 2

2. To form the plural of any outline ending in a mark of punctuation, double the last mark of punctuation. savings 2

3. To form the past tense of a regular verb, write a hyphen after the outline. used 6

4. Write / for the word ending *ness*. kindness 26

5. To show capitalization, draw a small curved line under the last letter of the outline. Bill 1

6. Write \ to indicate a period at the end of a sentence. 1

7. Write × to indicate a question mark. 1

8. Write > to indicate the end of a paragraph. 1

9. Write ! to indicate an exclamation mark. 5

10. Write = to indicate a dash. 5

11. Write = to indicate a hyphen. 5

12. To indicate solid capitalization, double the curved line underneath the last letter of the outline. 5

13. To indicate an underlined title, draw a solid line under the outline. 5

Miscellaneous